The MRP
and French
Foreign Policy

The MRP
and French
Foreign Policy

RUSSELL B. CAPELLE

FREDERICK A. PRAEGER, *Publisher*
New York

Published in the United States of America in 1963 by
Frederick A. Praeger, Inc., Publisher
64 University Place, New York 3, N.Y.

Manufactured in the United States of America

Foreword

When I first considered the MRP as a subject for study, I was advised to steer clear of the maze of French politics. The reader must judge the wisdom of my decision to rush in where scientific "angels" feared to tread.

There were certainly moments of doubt during the long period before my manuscript was sent to the publisher—a time span that was greatly affected by the obligations of a full fifteen-hour teaching schedule. Had it not been for the generous financial assistance of Norwich University, where I have been a member of the faculty for eight years, this book might never have seen the light.

My interest in France goes back many years. I remember, in my early years, being enamored of French names that my father brought back along with other memories when he returned from France with the AEF. My interest was preserved by French courses at Dartmouth, especially by the course under Professor Denoeu, whose book *La Vierge aux Yeux de Feu* recounted his experiences in World War I and helped to unfold for me the fullness, exactness, intricacies, and delicacies of the French language.

This interest was revived when I spent some nine months in France as an antiaircraft officer in 1944, having first seen its shores on D-Day on the Riviera. My wife and I had the opportunity to see France again briefly in the summer of 1949, but it was not until 1954 that I chose to plunge into the study of French politics. With some financial aid from Dartmouth, I spent three months carrying on very concentrated research in Paris (after a similar period at Harvard's Widener Library) and engaging in many interviews with party leaders and others (whose names are identified in Appendix A).

Very considerate treatment was accorded me by the party leaders whom I contacted. (Special thanks should go to Pierre Pflimlin, Georges Le Brun Kéris, and Jacques Mallet.) How, then, have I managed to be so critical of the MRP? Because, of course, we who are teachers are necessarily involved in criticism, with the hope that it will have constructive results. Perhaps some will say that I have not been critical enough. After mulling over some complimentary references I had made to the party leader Robert Schuman, a friend who read an early draft of the manuscript remarked caustically, "Did he love his mother?"

This study is confined almost entirely to the period between 1944 and June, 1954, since the MRP leaders Bidault and Schuman alternated as Minister of Foreign Affairs for these ten years (except for one month) and no MRP member has held that post since. However, an Epilogue traces the party's history to the present.

To the best of my knowledge, no other study of MRP foreign policy has been made, either in the United States or abroad. A glance at the Bibliography will indicate how few books relate, even in an indirect way, to the MRP. Most of the sources for this study are either newspapers, other periodicals, or public documents and party publications. Particular attention was devoted to *L'Aube*, *The New York Times*, and *The Times* (London). By far the greatest amount of information was derived from French periodicals, a complete search having been made through some of them, such as *Esprit*, for the period involved. (Part IV of the Bibliography indicates the time range within which periodicals were used.) The *Journal des Débats* of the National Assembly was also used extensively to reveal the activity and reactions of MRP deputies.

Further information was secured in 1954 through some attendance at the French National Assembly and through interviews with about twenty-five French political figures, about twenty of whom were leaders of the MRP. (A list of them is to be found in Appendix A.) Research was also carried on at the Bibliothèque Nationale, the Bibliothèque de Documentation Internationale Contemporaine, the Centre d'Études de Politique Étrangère, and the National Assembly Library. Much material was also obtained from the MRP Secretariat. Outside Paris, interviews were conducted by me with local MRP leaders in eastern and western France, and I attended for two days the National Congress of the MRP at Lille in May.

Since then, contact has been maintained with the MRP Secretariat, during a period when discordant elements like the rightists, led by Bidault, have been sloughed off. At the same time younger elements represented, for example, by Pflimlin and Lecanuet have come to the fore. Perhaps—just perhaps—in the doubtful days that lie ahead for the Fifth Republic, this party may be, as MRP ideology has always maintained, the "party of tomorrow."

The list in Appendix A gives some indication of those to whom I am indebted in France. In this country, I should like to express appreciation for significant assistance from members of the Department of Government of Boston University during the earlier stages of the manuscript: to Hubert Gibbs for his necessary pinpricks, to Andrew Gyorgy for his faith in my project at a critical stage, and to Pamela Wrinch for her constructive and specific criticisms.

Within the past year, my colleagues in history and government at Norwich University—specifically, Sidney Morse, Albert Norman, Eber Spencer, and Allan Nash—were kind enough to examine my manuscript and make very constructive suggestions. I suppose they will find that I have not quite followed all of them. I should like also to thank Mrs. Gary Atwood for her careful typing when time was of the essence. I have already thanked the University for its generous assistance.

Last—and, of course, by no means least—I wish to express my appreciation to my wife for her traveling companionship, her typing, and especially her tolerance over the long haul, which seemed at times without end.

—R. B. C.

September, 1962
Norwich University
Northfield, Vt.

Contents

The MRP
and French
Foreign Policy

Introduction : A Guide for the Reader

At the time of writing, early 1962, France is still deeply involved in the fears and hopes of the Western world. In a television interview in late December, 1961, the famed commentator Walter Lippmann said that he was more fearful about the fate of democracy in France, should there be no Algerian solution, than he was about the fate of Berlin. On the other hand, the hopes of the West for developing an economic offensive are deeply bound up with the expanding European Common Market. France, a member from the beginning, has found that the Market is clearly working to her own economic advantage.

How is the Mouvement Républicain Populaire connected with all this? Domestically, this "party of the Fourth Republic" sought consistently through the first ten years of its existence to maintain the middle ground in French politics in order to protect democracy from the threats of both political extremes. Internationally, the MRP identified itself from the first with the program of European integration; one of its leaders made the initial proposal for the creation of the European Coal and Steel Community; and a leader of the MRP continuously presided over the French Foreign Office for ten full years, thereby helping to preserve a remarkable continuity in French foreign policy.

It is true that, in contrast to its first ten years, the MRP has played little direct part in French government since 1954. But its leader, Pflimlin, was the last Premier of the Fourth Republic, having yielded power to De Gaulle because of the exigencies of the Algerian crisis in 1958. The party surprised skeptics by doing better than expected in maintaining its representation in the National Assembly of the Fifth Republic. In fact, Maurice Schumann, the voice of Free France in World War II and a past President of the MRP, held the significant post of President of the Assembly's Committee on Foreign Affairs in 1960. More recently, five MRP leaders held posts in De Gaulle's cabinet until they resigned in May, 1962, in protest against De Gaulle's concept of European federation.

This work is a case study of the efforts of a political party to

3

reconcile ideals with reality. The MRP, having achieved the support of too few, sought to be too much to too many. Although my main purpose is to determine, through detailed examination, the relative accuracy of this perhaps too-simple statement, other purposes are to examine the effect of personalities upon politics, the effect on party ideology of participation in government, the relation of religion to politics in France, and the increasing importance of foreign policy as a factor in the survival of French governments.

As the reader wades into the maze of French politics reflected in this study, he should keep certain basic questions in mind. Part One is concerned with determining how confined the sources of support and, separately, the centers of control of the MRP were. Since historical tradition means so much in France, we first examine briefly the "family history" of the MRP. Thereafter, because lack of *civisme* is such a handicap to the operations of French political life, it is important to consider whether the base of support of the MRP was too small to overcome this.

In Part Two, the basic question is whether the MRP sought to be "too much to too many." Was its ideology too complex, an ideology that opposed both capitalism and Communism, that embraced pluralism, and that centered on an international program of integration? Was its effort to treat problems on a world scale, under the doctrine that "peace is indivisible," too unrealistic? Was the MRP, on the other hand, too French for its own program, with its nationalistic support for the *status quo* in certain areas?

Finally, in Part Three, as we examine the tactics of the MRP in and out of parliament, we seek to determine whether party leaders were sufficiently skilled as politicians. Were they reasonably consistent among themselves, and steady enough in support of their various policies, especially at crucial moments? Were they, in short, too impractical to deal with that complicated and frustrating body the French parliament?

And yet, how realistic and practical should a political party be? Should the MRP have been more able to maneuver the "fifth estate" of pressure groups without submitting to it on occasion? It is possible that this would have significantly modified the rather amazing continuity of MRP ideology, especially of its core policy of European integration, for whose surprising progress at this early date the party can claim some large degree of credit.

PART ONE

I

Historical Background

The Mouvement Républicain Populaire, organized in 1944 and calling itself the "party of the Fourth Republic," might well have preferred to have been without ancestors. But a sense of history is strong in France, and as the most recent representative of French political Catholicism, the MRP could not divorce itself from its religious heritage, which was not one of unity in politics. At the party National Congress in 1950, a delegate alleged that one of the purposes of the MRP was to heal France of the wounds caused by the friction in the late eighteenth century between the *"Blancs"* and the *"Bleus"* over the drafting of the Civil Constitution of the Clergy by the Assembly of 1790. The former, who were old-order priests (*prêtres réfractaires*) mainly in the north and west of France, would not support the Civil Constitution.[1]

The cleavage between social Catholics and Christian democrats can be traced to this initial division of the French Church. As early as 1830, Lamennais, hailed by many as the founder of Christian democracy, led a group of Catholics toward the Left in politics. But some of his followers abandoned him, and, under the July Monarchy of the 1830's and 1840's, most French Catholics belonged to the conservative political alignment called the "resistance," as distinguished from the more progressive "movement." These included Montalembert and De Mun, founder of the Catholic labor circles. The early leaders of Christian democracy did not adapt themselves to the nineteenth century as well as the social-Catholic members of the Ralliement, for example, who were inspired by Pope Leo XIII (in his famous encyclical *Rerum Novarum* in 1891) to involve themselves in the problems of society.

Although in the aftermath of the Dreyfus Affair most of the political Left had been alienated from Catholicism at the beginning of the twentieth century, Marc Sangnier brought together a nucleus of Christian democrats to form a movement called

7

Sillon (Furrow). (At the death of Sangnier in 1950, Bidault referred to him as *"l'Initiateur"* of the MRP.) But again there was a gradual sliding to the Right. In 1910, Sangnier accepted the condemnation of *Sillon* by Pope Pius X, and he thereafter advocated the formation of *"une élite eclairée et courageuse"* capable of becoming a leader class. But in both respects he was moving toward social Catholicism and away from Christian democracy.[2]

Yet Sangnier did organize the Ligue de la Jeune République between 1910 and 1920. Still in existence in 1954, this group was further Left in political Catholicism than any except a few *"Chrétiens progressistes"* with whom it had ties. Its international policy was significant. Even before the creation of the League of Nations, the Jeune République favored a supranational society (in substance, if not in name), to be directed by popularly elected representatives of the member governments and possessing a police force. Sangnier sought to develop international contacts by initiating three international democratic congresses after World War I.

Despite its support for an international police force, the Jeune République was essentially pacifist, and it also firmly opposed French occupation of the Ruhr. It favored revision of the Treaty of Versailles and supported simultaneous reduction by all nations of all armaments, to be accompanied by a system of control over them.

The Parti Démocratique Populaire, founded in 1924, was more equivocal in its international policy. It favored a middle course between continued armament and unplanned disarmament, but in practice seemed to support preservation of armaments. Although professing to support the internationalism of Aristide Briand, the PDP later identified itself with the two-faced Laval policy of 1935–36. Yet the party was closely associated with the journal *L'Aube*, which, through the editorials of Bidault, expressed steady hostility to the capitulations and appeasements of the 1930's.

Within the PDP, there was an attempt to combine Christian democracy and social Catholicism. Its delegates in the National Assembly came as a rule from traditionally Right-wing districts; hence, if the party was Christian democratic in form, it was social Catholic in composition. Robert Schuman has indicated that the PDP should be distinguished from the MRP in that the former was not so closely linked to labor groups. While he and Le Brun

Kéris of the MRP leadership considered the division between social Catholics and Christian democrats an artificial one, other party leaders saw rather clear-cut distinctions. There does seem to be a definite contrast between the purposes and methods of these two branches of political Catholicism, and this contrast will be seen to have had a direct bearing on the formulation of the foreign policy of the MRP.

The gist of the distinction between Christian democrats and social Catholics is that the former seek to achieve social reforms for the masses through the direct participation of Catholics in politics in some form of party organization. In contrast, social Catholics believe that higher officials of the Church should take indirect political action to provide for the masses the amount of social reform considered advisable by the Catholic Right. In other words, they favor a hierarchical political organization, with control being exerted downward from the higher levels. Social Catholics believe that it is a function of the Church to inspire the enactment of social measures and to define the attitudes that others should have (as illustrated by stands they have taken at their periodic meetings, called *Semaines Sociales*). Paternalism is favored, and, in contrast to the emphasis on politics of individual Christian democrats, social Catholics give priority to the Church over political considerations.[3]

The composition and characteristics of the European "communities" that have been sponsored or supported by the MRP (to be discussed in Chapter 4) might be quite different according to whether they represented the ideals of Christian democracy or those of social Catholicism. If the latter were the case, there would be less likelihood of direct representation of the people of national groups in the legislative branches of these communities, and greater likelihood of influence exerted indirectly by the Pope and other high Church officials. Since the principal speakers on foreign policy at both party National Congresses of 1960 and 1961 supported election of deputies by universal suffrage to a single European parliamentary assembly, it appears that at least in this respect the MRP has retained its Christian-democratic quality.[4]

Despite various compromises, it is quite clear that Christian democracy had increased its influence by 1940 in France as a whole, if not within the National Assembly itself. But World War II brought new schisms into the ranks of French political Catholicism. The Rightist *fidèles* (faithful to Pétain) were opposed to the Leftist *compagnons* of the Resistance. Perhaps it was in order to overcome its equivocal record during the Vichy regime that the Church threw much of its weight behind support for the MRP in 1945 and 1946. But it is unlikely that any party could reconcile all the political views contained within the spectrum of political Catholicism.

The Mouvement Républicain Populaire is a party of external origin, having developed outside politics in the narrow sense of the word. Created as it was by the dynamics of the Resistance and, in part, by the influence of the Church, it is interesting that the leaders of this group chose *Mouvement* for the first word of its name. Not that anyone would confuse the Resistance of the World War II period with the Rightist political Catholic resistance of the nineteenth century. But there may have been some intention to associate the new party with the more progressive movement in French politics of that century.

Many leaders of the MRP, including Maurice Schumann, Georges Bidault, Colin, and Moulin, had been active in the overseas organization of the Free French and also in the formation of the National Resistance Council. Most of the members of the PDP and the Jeune République had refused to vote constituent power to Pétain in 1940, but it was the MRP that, in 1944, took the only effective step ventured by any Resistance group to transform itself into a political party. The leaders of the MRP believed that the Communist Party should not be allowed to stand as the only political revolutionary movement in France. A vacuum had been created by the inertia of other former political groups in France, and the MRP stepped into that vacuum.[5]

Relation of Party Structure to
Foreign Policy

A Regional Party

In succeeding chapters, a close examination will be made of the difficulties faced by the MRP in attempting to attain a series of complicated objectives through its program of European integration, its policy in the East-West struggle, and its policy toward the French Union and North Africa. First, however, attention must be given to fundamental handicaps to be found within the internal structure of the MRP. Its keystone policy of European integration involved clear-cut invasions of sovereignty that a people as nationalistic as the French were most hesitant to accept. A political party that sought to accomplish such a goal needed the broadest possible contacts with the French nation. These the MRP in no way had. Later, it will be seen that, because of the narrowness of its contacts within France, the party could not very well make its influence felt by means of the press, let alone the business world. Most important, however, was the basic fact that the MRP was a regional party.

The predecessors of the MRP were, if anything, more narrowly regional in their strength than the MRP itself. Except for its leader, De Ribes, the Parti Démocratique Populaire drew its fifteen deputies either from the west of France or from Alsace-Lorraine. Its supporters, as well as those of the Jeune République, were mainly confined to twelve departments, which are also the *môles* (strongholds) of the MRP.

Although it received 5 million votes in the election of 1946, the MRP had only 350,000 adherents who were reliable party members. The geographical representation of the party in the French

National Assembly between 1947 and 1954 was quite unbalanced and totaled eighty-odd seats, or about one-sixth of the entire body.

In 1946, when the MRP got 25.9 per cent of the votes cast, it was really strong only in Normandy, Brittany, Poitou, Champagne, Alsace and the "annexed" part of Lorraine, some few mountainous areas, and the urbanized department of Nord. In many of these areas—for example, in Alsace—the local priest, the regional journal, and the town *maire* were all in the MRP fold. Hence, the idea of having another party allegiance did not occur to the average Catholic peasant. But in Alsace, most of the Protestants have been Gaullists since 1947 because of the apparent clericalism of the MRP. Elsewhere, there is a band of departments in the center of France, from Charente in the west to Haute-Marne in the east, where the MRP is very weak, as the Assistant Secretary-General himself admitted. This band of weakness lies just above Haute-Loire, the home department of Bidault.

It would have been difficult enough for the MRP to lead a "European movement," controlling as it did only a relatively small number of the ninety departments in France. It was even more difficult in view of the fact that the party's greatest strength lay in a few of those mountainous areas of France that were strongly clerical (composed of Catholics who took their religion seriously) or else in the far east or far west, especially in Brittany. (The former province of Brittany was farthest removed geographically, and to a great extent in spirit, from that part of Europe directly involved in the program of integration.) The local interests of the predominantly rural voters in these MRP strongholds were quite divorced, at least in their own minds, from European problems, and it is hard for the leadership of a party to disregard the inclinations of its strongest supporters. The MRP lacked sufficient strength in urban areas, which are, as a rule, more inclined to be sensitive to the currents of international politics than rural areas.

Of course, it is possible for a party with only regional strength and with a conservative, nationally minded electorate to prosecute an internationalist policy if it has leaders with a degree of political prestige who are themselves internationally minded. Pflimlin and Schuman of the MRP, coming as they do from the border provinces of Alsace and Lorraine, were internationally minded, but Schuman did not have enough political influence with the French parliament. Teitgen, a perennial President of the party, owed his allegiance to the conservative, clerical voters of Brittany. De Menthon came from the mountainous department of Haute-Savoie, and Bidault from Haute-Loire, almost the geographical center of France. These last two leaders, especially Bidault, had considerable political prestige. But, just as American isolationism in the past has been predominantly located in the Middle West, so also is nationalism especially strong in mountainous departments of France like Haute-Savoie or in centrally located departments like Haute-Loire. It was Bidault who removed himself from the MRP after 1958 because of his extremely nationalistic approach to the Algerian question.

Daniel Lerner has demonstrated, however, in his contribution to *France Defeats the EDC*, that there is no clear geographical pattern showing border areas for such a thing as European integration and central areas against it; in fact, more of its opponents come from border areas. A clearer dividing line would be that from Rouen to Marseille, although the richer, more dynamic industrial area northeast of that line was more opposed to the European Community than the static area to the southwest.

In the past, there has been a traditionally close relationship between the peasantry and Catholicism, and a preference for rural areas even seems to be incorporated within the constitution of the MRP. The party Statute provides for the allotment of delegates to the National Congress by a rule of "progression" that gives less than proportionate weight to the larger departmental federations and more than proportionate representation, as a result, to federations in less populous rural departments. According to MRP leaders, the use of this rule of progression did not lead in itself to provincialism, or a greater stress on rural than on urban areas. One leader contended that this rule was necessary to reflect provincial differences, which are very striking in France. Nevertheless, it appears that, by incorporating such a provision in its Statute, the MRP did to that extent insulate itself against urban influence.

The MRP has professed to be a political movement serving all groups in the French nation, and has maintained that, in contrast with other French political parties, it is not a "class" party. But its geographical centers of strength are so limited that it would be difficult for the MRP to maintain any proper contact with all groups in France. As for freedom from class allegiance, the party appears on the contrary to be primarily confined to a social milieu that might best be described as that portion of the French lower middle class composed of practicing Catholics.

This milieu is to be found primarily in the rural areas referred to above. The MRP is not conservative enough in political and economic matters to satisfy most of the upper class or the *grande bourgeoisie* (upper middle class) in the cities, most of whom are closely connected with business. On the other hand, the MRP is too conservative to draw the bulk of its support from the lower class. Nevertheless, François Goguel credited the party with having as much support from labor in 1954 as the Socialists had or as the RPF of De Gaulle had at the peak of its career. He also noted, however, that the MRP was moving toward conservatism and had in general replaced, in its local strongholds, the moderate or conservative parties of the Third Republic. A student of Catholic parties in Europe has declared that "Catholicism and conservatism are expressions of an identical community type," and this seems to hold true as well for the Christian-democratic wing of Catholicism. The Christian-democratic vote has generally grown at the expense of the conservative parties.[1]

While it had not extended its geographical base to any appreciable extent, the MRP appeared to have strengthened its local positions in early 1954. In some cases, at least, the change seems to have been connected with the party's consistent support of the principle of European integration. In 1953, it had gained in Alsace, Champagne, and Brittany, and in early 1954, despite a contest with a coalition that opposed the EDC, the MRP secured a significant seat in the National Assembly from Saumur, which was followed by the victory of Mme. Peyrolles in the greater Paris department of Seine-et-Oise. In this election, she was the only candidate to come out clearly for European integration. Shortly thereafter, in May, Sauvage of the MRP won a victory in Maine-et-Loire that represented a clear decision for the European Defense Community, since his opponent was definitely against the proposed treaty. Here was evidence of gains both in urban and rural departments, and, in the industrialized department of Pas-de-Calais, the MRP candidate at this time was the only one to gain votes for his party. Despite these gains in early 1954, however, the MRP still remained a regional party, having real strength in only about twelve of the ninety French metropolitan departments.

A *Catholic Party*

One not too familiar with French political history might wonder why it would be a handicap to be classified as the "Catholic party" in a nation as Catholic as France. Of course in some ways it was an advantage. There was a certain tenacity, devotion to doctrine, and party loyalty within the MRP that may have been related to the religiosity of its members. An anticlerical Radical Socialist from Burgundy commented that many opponents of the MRP were afraid the party would *keep* its promises. But there is a general political disadvantage for the MRP in being identified as the Catholic party. France is Catholic on the surface, but there are relatively few practicing Catholics in France. Anticlericalism is a strong political force, especially in the Radical Socialist and Socialist parties (as well as the Communist Party, of course). The MRP had sought uniqueness by calling itself the party of the Fourth Republic, but it was given an unsolicited and unwanted unique position when many identified it as the Catholic party.

Implicit in this position was a particular danger to the party's foreign policy. Although, because of its composition, it had close ties with international Catholic organizations sponsoring European integration, it was at the same time subject to the charge that such a movement, if successful, would lead to a "black Europe" under the domination of the Vatican. (Black is the usual color of vestments of the Catholic hierarchy; thus, "black Europe" suggests to the minds of many Europeans a Europe under the control of the Papacy, which had reached the peak of its temporal power in the Middle Ages.) Would there be a new "Saint-Empire" led by the Pope?

The principal warning of the danger of a Vatican Europe came from Joseph Hours, one of the founders of the MRP, who sought to develop a chain of continuity linking the Burgundians of the eleventh century with the Christian democrats and specifically with the MRP. Burgundian clericalism and provincialism, said Hours, had been opposed to French nationalism, and he compared such hostility to centralization with MRP success in "provincial" Brittany and Alsace.

In a long journalistic controversy during 1950 with Étienne Borne, an intellectual leader of the MRP, Hours contended that in its foreign policy the MRP reflected an old tradition of mistrust of sovereign states, and noted that Borne was most disturbed at the accusation that the party was unpatriotic. Borne replied that the MRP had no historical connection with pre-Revolutionary political movements—neither with Burgundian clericalism, which had opposed Armagnac nationalism, nor with the Sainte-Ligue, which had opposed centralization of power in the state. He added that the subordination of the state to a higher value such as the European idea should not be called antistatism.

When Borne argued that Christianity had never been solely under the control of the Popes, who had been in competition with the Holy Roman emperors, Hours changed his tactics and declared that the Holy Roman Empire lived in the memory of the Germans more than of any other people. The principal check to the Hapsburgs, he said, had been at the hands of the French, and resistance to Europe had been a fundamental doctrine in French history. Hours reminded his readers that an international of Catholic parties was neither strange nor new, having been a Hapsburg idea up until 1918.

In his book *France Against Herself*, Herbert Luethy charged Hours with "indiscriminate jumbling," but admitted that there was a grain of truth in what he had said. The single-minded Hours could not make a case against Monnet—the master planner of such steps in European integration as the European Coal and Steel Community—since Monnet was quite unclerical by inclination. But Hours might have been much closer to the truth in questioning as he did the motives of Robert Schuman, who happened to come from Lorraine, the center of the later Carolingian empire. When questioned on this issue of Schuman's motives, a former close assistant of his, who served as a French member of the Council of Europe staff in 1954, was quite equivocal in his answer.[2]

In addition to the alarmist opinions of this disaffected former member of the MRP (Hours), occasional pronouncements of party leaders themselves, especially of Teitgen, gave some cause for concern about a "black Europe." In a 1950 speech, Teitgen, President of the MRP, referred to the "imperious" necessity to construct Europe in a manner that would save "Christian humanism." Three years later, he spoke of making a Europe that would remain the "guardian of the Christian sources on which is founded all au-

thentic civilization." ("Christian" here means "Catholic.") One
critic saw in this an exaltation of "indissoluble communities" over
engagements qui passent, reflecting a social-Catholic preference for
institutions over contracts. By this mystique, said Detraz, the MRP
(which he called a "party of jurists") was rejoining the tradition of
political Catholicism.

In general, however, the MRP gave little justification to those
who feared a "black Europe." Bidault was primarily a Gallican in
supporting the independence of France from the Church. Only the
unorthodox Senator Hamon had fallen under the influence of
Hours in suspecting the motives of his colleagues in the party (from
which he was later excluded). Teitgen himself sought on occasion
to emphasize that European integration was not a Rightist policy.
Le Brun Kéris believed that the violent opposition of Hours to the
MRP had unbalanced his thinking. Another leader accused Hours
of being an *intellectuel fermé* who, failing to accomplish anything
himself, resorted to negative criticism of those who did. Nonparty
Goguel thought Hours ridiculous in seeking to malign the patriotism of the MRP by calling it "ultramontane."

But Hours was not alone. Although many Europeans left religion at home when they talked about integration of Europe, unfortunately for the MRP, its anticlerical opponents neither allowed
the party to leave religion at home nor the religious issue to lie dor-
mant at home. Although both Blum and Guesde, leaders of the
Socialists, had attacked the spirit of anticlericalism, the MRP-
Socialist alliance that existed up to 1950 soon became strained over
the issue. And the Socialists were not the only opponents of the
MRP in this respect. The anticlerical Radical Socialists had also
taken a harsh stand against the MRP as early as September, 1950,
because of the party's alleged intransigency on educational reform
and the church-school issue. Nearly half of the MRP parliamentary
group after the 1951 elections came from departments where the
issue of church-state relations was paramount. This had a fundamental effect upon the general voting behavior of representatives in
parliament.

Meanwhile, the Gaullists were indirectly encouraging the MRP
on the church-school issue in order to keep the conflict with the
Socialists alive. By the autumn of 1953, Mollet and other Socialist
leaders were seeking to build a new movement of "economic and

social democracy" to fight against the Christian democracy of "Adenauer and the MRP" (note the order of precedence), and Mollet sought also to bring anticlericals among the practicing Catholics into the movement.

At an early stage in the MRP campaign for European integration, the Socialists had opposed leaving French foreign policy in the hands of such a devout Catholic as Schuman. In 1950, Mollet warned against *"la politique Vaticane,"* and another Socialist, Viviani, criticized Bidault for seeking to create an "international conscience." During the National Assembly debate on the European Defense Community in February, 1952, the Socialist leader Moch declared that the EDC reminded him of the empire of Charlemagne or perhaps of that of Louis *"le Débonnaire,"* since a strong hand like Charlemagne's would be missing. Again, at the Socialist Congress the following year, Moch said: "We refuse to join a crusade for the resuscitation of the Europe of Charlemagne, Napoleon, or Hitler. That Europe which may be a Vatican Europe and will certainly be a Europe under German hegemony is the worst of all possible Europes." He received an ovation from the Congress for this statement. In 1954, when Moch was in the strong tactical position of *rapporteur* of the Committee on Foreign Affairs of the National Assembly, he opposed an EDC that would be so under the influence of Catholics. Finally, at the special Socialist Congress called in May, 1954, to consider the problem of the EDC, factions led by Naegelen, Daniel Mayer, and Moch opposed the army plan partly because of fears of a Vatican Europe.[3]

Those who raised the specter of a "black Europe" were connecting the idea of Vatican control of Europe with that of German hegemony under the leadership of Adenauer, the Christian Democrat. They failed to give proper consideration to the fact that the aging Adenauer had an increasingly tenuous grasp on the reins of control in Germany. Such fears, however, were enough in themselves to act as a handicap to the foreign policy of the MRP, especially since certain Socialist leaders took the stand noted above. For the tactical position of the Socialists in parliament was very strong when the EDC Treaty came up before the National Assembly for a final decision in the summer of 1954.[4]

Just how Catholic is the Catholic party? While many nominal Catholics are opposed to the MRP, there is also, among the practic-

ing Catholics (Chrétiens), a distinction between the younger
Catholic clergy of the rural east and west, who lean toward the
MRP, and city priests and bishops. The latter are more inclined to
favor wealthy bourgeois interests represented in other parties whose
ties to business are closer than those of the MRP. Well aware of
the splits in French Catholicism, the leaders of the party excluded
Chrétien from its name. The MRP keeps itself open to all faiths
and has had a few Protestants and Jews in its midst. The experienced political observers Fauvet and Goguel seem to agree that the
MRP is "no vassal of the Church," its religious inclination being
clearly evident only in its program for "freedom of education."[5]

There is a particular reason for MRP wariness about being too
closely associated with Catholicism, and that is the split between
social Catholics and Christian democrats discussed above. Michel
Darbon, in his history of political Catholicism, declared that Right
(social) Catholics hate the Christian democrats more than they do
the anticlericals. Yet the two branches of Catholicism in the MRP
are so interwoven in the public mind that sometimes the party is
referred to as Christian democratic and sometimes as Christian social. Hours, also, had confused the two branches, charging that
there was a "black international" of social Catholics at the end of
the nineteenth century and attacking the "founders of Christian
democracy." And Borne, in denying some part of the historical
connections of the MRP with the past, was to that extent denying
a connection of the party with the long development of social
Catholicism in France.

Borne had become engaged in a controversy with the political
writer Maurice Duverger, who had said in 1950 that the "West will
die because it seeks to draw from Christianity a state doctrine, although Christianity only contains a doctrine of resistance to the
state." Although Borne charged Duverger with oversimplification,
making general a statement applicable perhaps to a totalitarian
state, the latter's prestige was such that pronouncements of this
sort tended to increase suspicion of Church-connected parties.[6]
This was especially true if a connection were made in the public's
mind with pluralism, a part of the MRP political philosophy.
Pluralism dates back to the Middle Ages when the embryonic
states were unequal competitors for power, and it incorporates the
idea that a division of power is necessary among the spontaneous

and natural groups that make up society. According to the plural-
ists, no single body such as the state was considered fit to represent
the community as a whole.

A Centralized Party

As we shall see in Part Two, the MRP support for the participation of producers, consumers, and laborers in the economic aspects
of European integration represented at least in part an application
of the party doctrine of pluralism. Similarly, in its domestic program, the MRP sought to develop the family's participation in
public activities. Moreover, as early as 1945, some of the proposals
made by the party in the constitutional convention had reflected a
pluralistic concept of parliament. For example, the MRP favored
the parliamentary representation of various social and economic
groups, such as family associations. According to MRP doctrine,
there is an organic unity to these groups, which are not created by
law but grow naturally. The state is considered to be only the pro-
tector and regulator of such groups, which, according to the plural-
ists, are the fundamental source of power.

Yet in supporting pluralism, the MRP was opposing the French
conception of a centralized state, a radically antipluralist conception. Primarily as a result of this centralization, France has failed
to develop much spontaneous local community life. Where spon-
taneity exists in local groups, it leads toward the development of
pluralism. However, one of the particular weaknesses of the MRP,
in spite of this facet of its ideology, has been its failure to foster
enough local social and political activity to make a spontaneous
community life possible. The party fell in step with France, therefore, as it fell out of step with its own doctrine.

Francisque Gay, one of the earlier leaders of the MRP, was very
critical of this failure of the party, as well as of the PDP before it,
to maintain direct contacts with public opinion and to stress the
civic spirit. The MRP had developed its theoretical support for
pluralism only in respect to the family group. Neither the MRP
nor the PDP, said Gay, had created enough local units. In the
1930's, he had represented the whole Left Bank in Paris for the
PDP.

This weakness of the MRP is mainly a reflection of the fact that it had been from the beginning a centralized party. Such an authority as Gordon Wright has seen fit to call it monolithic, a term usually reserved for Communist parties.[7] The centralization of control in the hands of a few leaders (however much they might disagree among themselves) allows scant leeway for the decentralization of power implicit in the idea of pluralism. Lecourt, parliamentary leader of the MRP in 1954, sought to resolve the contradiction between theory and practice by drawing a distinction between deconcentration and decentralization (in respect to power within society rather than within the party). The MRP, he said, favored deconcentration, but was typically French in its hostility to decentralization, if the latter meant transfer of political control down to the department level in France. According to Lecourt, the party was enthusiastic about local or regional planning in social and economic matters, but was skeptical about provincial autonomy.

Can it be said that the MRP has had an oversupply of doctrine? Even if this is true, much of the doctrine has taken the form of misty ideology that has not been down to earth enough. In this respect, the MRP is certainly distinct from the Communists. The Communists have a solid doctrine based on tactical and practical considerations but nonetheless apparently unswerving in its eventual goal. In 1947, Gilson, MRP member of the Académie Française, asked whether it was really fortunate to have a codified set of ideas such as the Communists have. It was, he believed, a pattern of reasoning that finds peace in its own abdication. Action Française had had such a systematic doctrine, he said; should the MRP follow the example of that extremist organization? Yet if certain MRP leaders cast scorn on the inflexibility of Communist doctrine, it was not long before they themselves were to establish quite as inflexible a doctrine in the support for European integration.

Duverger has drawn an interesting as well as provocative parallel between the origins of the MRP and the Bolshevists: Both had their foundations in an underground movement, although the two movements were quite distinct in character. The MRP was quick to develop a centralized organization more similar to the pattern of the formerly well-knit French Communist Party than to that of any other French political group. The MRP seems to have been from the start a party rather than a movement, despite its name. The Communists, with their strong centralized organization, had more respect for the MRP than for any other political party in France.[8]

Duverger has made a careful distinction between parties of direct and indirect structure, centralized and decentralized parties, and parties of external and internal origin. The MRP has a direct structure, perhaps as a result of its desire to imitate Continental socialist methods. (In contrast to the British Labour Party, based indirectly upon trade unions, the French Socialists have followed the direct pattern, claiming the loyalty of their adherents without the presence of any intermediate centers of loyalty. In this respect, the MRP is similar to the French Socialists.) With regard to the degree of centralization of control, Christian-democratic parties in general seem to straddle the fence between the pattern of bourgeois decentralized parties and that of social centralized parties. But parties of external origin, such as the MRP, tend to be more centralized than those of internal origin.[9]

On the surface, policy is supposedly created by combined discussion and decisions on various levels of the MRP party structure. Besides the local sections and department federations, there is a National Committee, as well as a National Congress, which meets once a year. The sections are composed of ten or more adherents each and engage in discussions, formulate resolutions, and carry on educational and propaganda activity. The federations are the main continuous organs of the party, however, each being composed of five or more sections and of at least 100 members. All adherents eighteen years old or more qualify for the right to vote in party conclaves. Candidates for political office are named, and, by secret ballot, federation congresses choose delegates to the National Congress, which any adherent may attend but where only delegates may vote.

Members of parliament usually have a rather minor role in parties of external origin. But this is not true of the MRP, and in this respect the party differs as well from the French Socialist Party. In December, 1951, the Executive Committee of the Socialist Party was given the sole right to determine whether to refuse a vote of confidence, regardless of the wishes of 106 Socialist members of the National Assembly. Again in May, 1954, a special Socialist Congress decided that "discipline of voting" should apply to party support for the EDC in the National Assembly; deputies were to vote strictly according to the decisions of the Congress.[10]

In contrast, although the MRP is quite centralized, the influence of its members in parliament is more than proportionate to their numbers in party councils. As Secretary-General Colin himself explained in 1954, the MRP believes that for reasons of strategic control the Secretary-General should not be a member of the Government (at least not coincidentally with the party President), but he should be a *parlementaire*. The National Committee, said Colin, had been criticized at times for having too many parliamentary members; the smaller Executive Commission, on the other hand, had been reproached for not having enough.

The MRP leaders who in effect formulated party foreign policy were either ministers in the Government or members of parliament. Between 1944 and 1954, the principal MRP leaders were Robert Schuman, Bidault, De Menthon, Teitgen, Letourneau, Maurice Schumann,* Lecourt, Borne, Pflimlin, and Buron.[11] Except for Étienne Borne, they were—some of them for a considerable time—members of either one of the chambers of parliament. Many of them had also been members of one or more of the numerous governments that had been formed since 1945. As a group, except for Schuman, they were relatively young and politically experienced only in the postwar period, compared to leaders of other French political parties. Although advanced in both years and political experience, Schuman did not seem to profit too much by this experience in his dealings with parliament.

In the lower echelons, not even the militants among party adherents were able to carry any appreciable weight, whether they expressed themselves through the sections, federations, or National Congresses. (As is the case with other French parties, there is a great difference between the number of MRP adherents and the number of those who vote for the party at the polls.) In 1954, according to the MRP Secretariat, the number of *cotisants* (card-carrying adherents who could be chosen as voting delegates at party assemblies) was barely more than 50,000. In short, foreign policy was created by a very small per cent of the supporters of the party.

If the MRP pretended to be a *mouvement*, then the "movers and shakers" who led in the search for ways to develop European integration were few in number. Since they were so few, one would think they would have done everything possible to publicize their

---

* Careful distinction must be made between Robert Schuman and Maurice Schumann.

program in order to compensate. But one of the most justifiable criticisms of the Schuman policy was that there was no widespread campaign to explain the European idea and the sacrifices it would entail to the French people or even to the "omnipotent" parliament. MRP President Teitgen asked in April, 1954, how many of those who criticized the EDC had read the Treaty, but the MRP had not exerted itself very much to make this possible. Perhaps the party's demand in early 1954 for a referendum on the EDC was a belated attempt to make up for its failure to educate public opinion up until then.[12] Much of the reason for this failure lay in the excessive centralization of control within the MRP.

A Case Study in Centralization

Perhaps the best illustration of the centralized character of the MRP is to be found in the ways in which party political activity, at the levels of sections and federations, is regulated from above. The National Statutes of the MRP provide that party meetings within a federation must be authorized by the controlling body of the federation in question. For a member of the party to participate in other meetings, he must take the advice of the president of the federation in whose area the meeting is to be held. Any discord is to be resolved by the National Executive Committee.[13]

Article 51 of the Statutes is important in this connection. It provides that members of the Mouvement may express their thoughts (through the usual channels) on condition that they conform to the decisions of the National Congress, National Committee, Executive Commission, and, if deputies or senators are involved, the appropriate parliamentary *groupe*. (That, it might be said parenthetically, is a big order.) On the other hand, the Statute specifically forbids members of the Mouvement to disseminate propaganda within the Mouvement for the benefit of an outside organization, without first having obtained the authorization of the Executive Commission. In Article 53, provision was made for a special commission of "discipline and arbitration" to handle troublesome cases.

Hence, four party bodies may determine certain activities of party members. All four bodies disproportionately reflect the will of national government officials who are members of the party. At

National Congresses, party members in the Government or parliament may vote regardless of whether or not they are official delegates. At least one-third of the National Committee is composed of all present or former members of the Government and parliament. The same preponderance of national government politicians is found in both the Executive Commission and the parliamentary group, which together compose a sort of interlocking directorate.[14]

The formal regulations in the MRP Statutes prescribe certain local activities of party members and at the same time proscribe others. A striking illustration of this centralized control occurred in early 1954 in the exclusion from the party of André Denis, a member of the National Assembly. Directly involved was the MRP requirement that the party rank and file support its policies toward the French Union and European integration. Simonnet's report to the National Committee in the name of the Commission on Discipline called attention to the fact that in the National Congress of May, 1953, after a period of free debate, the motions on Indochina and general foreign policy had been adopted unanimously except for six and three votes, respectively. All party candidates for the National Assembly, before their election, were required to accept the terms of Article 51 of the Statutes, restricting their political activity. It was the decision of the Commission that Denis had not kept to this commitment. It found that he had fought against these resolutions of the party Congress in the press; and in meetings opposing MRP policy on the EDC and Indochina, he was found to have slandered the leaders of the party. In fact, he had attempted to create a division in the party only three days after the Congress had ended.[15]

At the Paris Congress of 1953, MRP President Teitgen had declared that no conviction had been *tenue en bride* (bridled) within the party. "We do not have such a thing as official and pre-established truth," he said. It was in the Denis affair six months later that this declaration was put to a practical test. When the chips were down, the MRP certainly prized unity and discipline. That Denis had violated the voting discipline in the National Assembly was not, according to the Commission on Discipline, the determining element. It was rather the combination of his attitude of open rebellion and his action outside the MRP that led the Commission to its decision. An attempt had been made to get him to renounce such activities, but he had continued to participate in meetings with Communists and members of other political groups.[16]

In the final analysis, Teitgen and Bidault based the exclusion of Denis on his basic hostility to the EDC. He had, in contrast, clearly supported the ECSC, and the EDC was a step in European integration that many others in the party had grudgingly accepted as a rather bitter pill. There was considerable adverse criticism in the press of this action taken against Denis by the MRP, and, as a matter of fact, there was much dissension in the party and difference of opinion even within the Commission on Discipline over the wisdom of such a step. Perhaps this illustrates the high degree of intellectual freedom demanded by the French, which is often a divisive and sometimes a destructive influence in French politics. But it also illustrates the centralization of control in the MRP, which at times prevented a certain necessary degree of flexibility. A similar reflection of the centralized character of the MRP was found in the later expulsion of senator Leo Hamon from the party.

Double Pensants: *Dualism in Party Foreign Policy*

Thus, whatever its good intentions, the MRP labored under certain handicaps. Its electorate was quite limited, it was only one of six important parties in the French National Assembly, its religious connections caused complications, and for a *mouvement*, its directorate was quite concentrated. But, of course, this last characteristic is not so unusual; as Duverger has said, all parties are oligarchic. More important, however, was the fact that even within the party there was often too little observance by the leadership or heed by the "followership" of the policy decisions the MRP saw fit to make.

Through its centralization of control, the MRP preserved to outward appearances a surprising degree of cohesion. But a closer examination reveals a striking dualism within the party in its development of foreign policy. This split between theory and practice, between words and deeds, should not be called hypocrisy since it was not always conscious. Moreover, it was unlike ethical dualism, characterized by one standard of conduct for one's own group and a different one for others. For there were two forms of dualism within the party. On the one hand, there was a contrast between official party support for European integration and the reluctance and hesitations of certain party leaders in the Government when they had the chance to put party policy into effect. On the other hand, there was the contrast between the official MRP emphasis on foreign policy and the relative disregard for foreign policy evident in the actual proceedings of party Congresses, as well as in the meetings of federations and sections. For example, the MRP as a party stood firmly behind the program of European integration and accepted compromises in internal politics to preserve its continuity. But the active interest of the party rank and file was essential for the success of such a program. The French people could not be forced into support of European integration, and, in the long run, their support would certainly be needed for its success. If the MRP did not succeed in stimulating enthusiasm for European integration and interest in foreign policy in general, even within its own ranks, there was little likelihood that it could lead France as a whole into support for Europe.

As for the contrast between official party policy and the hesitations and equivocations of certain party leaders in the Government, proper account must be taken of the position of these leaders. It is one thing to run a risk in wording resolutions at party Congresses and another thing for MRP members of the Government to risk acting on such resolutions. The function of congresses is to preserve party doctrine, and, in the case of the MRP, another function was to keep the party, nominally at least, to the Left in its foreign policy. For example, the initial brochure of the MRP, published in 1945, called attention to the historic struggle for collective security waged by the PDP, its predecessor and announced that the MRP would "never agree to a policy of 'blocs,'" since blocs were considered to be potentially, if not fundamentally, aggressive.

It is unlikely that the party mystique could have survived unblemished through ten successive years of participation in the Government. At times, some MRP leaders were quick to seize the initiative in pursuance of their ideology, as did Schuman in announcing his Plan in 1950 (one of the purposes of which was to make it less necessary for France to adhere to the East or the West bloc). But they usually had to be more circumspect because of their positions of responsibility in the Government. Although Bidault made the observation—as an editorialist in *L'Aube* in 1950—that one should "row against the current" in political affairs, he destroyed some of the effect of this statement when he said that this tendency in individuals would operate as a balance against the policy they "must" practice.[17] Actually, as foreign minister Bidault often followed the current of political tradition rather than row against it, finding historical arguments for what often seemed to be an opportunistic personal policy.

Who wishes to be an angel in politics, said the political commentator Fauvet, acts the fool. Denis, before he was excluded from the party, put it another way: "One doesn't get out of a thicket at a gallop." Fauvet noted that there are two types of conflicts in every political movement: between thought and action and between *cadre* and *clientèle*. "*Quand on agit,*" he said, "*on trahit un peu.*" In 1950, *L'Aube* attempted to reassure those on the MRP Left wing who were troubled about preserving the distinction between the party as a whole and the members in the Government or parliament by arguing that participation in the Government was a guarantee that MRP doctrine would not be neglected by party leadership.[18]

Despite this guarantee, there was procrastination, if not neglect, to be attributed to the party's leadership. Even the apparently enthusiastic federalism of Teitgen wavered before the 1952 appeal to the Consultative Assembly by Spaak of Belgium for action toward the creation of a European political authority. Teitgen and De Menthon did, however, take an active part in the drafting of a proposed constitution for such an EPC in the fall of the year. But with respect to the European Defense Community, the cleavage between official party policy and that expressed by MRP leaders in the Government seemed to grow in 1952–53. Through resolutions of its Congresses and stands taken by its National Committee, the MRP, from the time of the signing of the treaty, had supported the EDC as an essential step in European integration. But it was not until October, 1953, that the party announced publicly that it would withdraw from the Government if the EDC were rejected.

One month later, in November, 1953, Bidault finally took a definite stand as Minister of Foreign Affairs in support of the EDC. He stood up in the National Assembly to say, "Without fear of displeasure nor desire for pleasure I speak my conscience." The world had not been promised, said Bidault, to those who hesitate (the shoe would seem to fit him); what was needed was a policy other than a choice between two dangers—*folle croisade* or *mortel repliement*. Perhaps the strain of committing himself so clearly for the EDC, as well as the strain of his office, was too much for him. In any event, Bidault had a fainting spell during his speech, and, when the session was resumed, Maurice Schumann read the rest of it.[19] Because of this turn of events, much of the possible effect of the original speech was lost on the Assembly.

Once Bidault had finally crossed his Rubicon, it appeared that the MRP was clearly committed to the EDC. Pflimlin gave it his outspoken support when he unsuccessfully sought the presidency of the National Assembly in December. In March, 1954, the MRP became the first party to ask its members in the Government to demand a debate on the EDC without delay. In the spring election campaigns in Seine-et-Oise and Brittany, party candidates seemed to profit from their stands in favor of the EDC. Nevertheless, the delays on this issue had been costly for the party, and its leaders in the Government were still inclined in 1954 to procrastinate in bringing the EDC issue to a head.

There was a continuing contrast in early 1954 between the official stand of the MRP and the attitude of Bidault as Minister of Foreign Affairs—for instance, over the important issue of German unity. At the Congress of 1952, Alfred Coste-Floret, reporting on the official party foreign policy, had declared that the MRP was not opposed to the idea of unification of Germany, since it would destroy the spirit of irredentism if consummated, but he had insisted that such unity be sought only within the "bosom" of Europe. When Bidault represented France as Minister of Foreign Affairs at the Berlin Conference of February, 1954, he declared that a unified Germany must follow free elections. But Bidault went on to contradict the 1952 pronouncement of Coste-Floret when he said that a liberty of choice must be extended to a new united Germany, which could not be manacled by the prior commitments of West Germany. France does not, said Bidault, "demand as a condition of German unification the entry of a united Germany into the European community, but refuses as well to allow an opposite prior condition." Regardless of which approach was more realistic, this is another illustration of the presence of a continuing dualism within the MRP.

It is difficult to escape the conclusion that many of the leaders of the MRP belong to that numerous group of individuals in politics whom Domenach, editor of *Esprit*, called the *double pensants* (double-thinkers)—who profess one policy while practicing another. Much of the reason for this, of course, lies in the fact that the leaders in the Government had to deal directly with parliament. Its nature had not changed much from what it was before 1848, as described by De Tocqueville: "One must have lived a long time amid parties . . . to understand how far men may drive each other to act against their own designs and how far the fate of the world may be determined not only by but against the wills of those who influence it, as a kite is driven by the contrary action of the wind and its own tail." In June, 1950, on the eve of his defeat as Premier, Bidault had declared that except where a *coup d'état* was involved, every government was necessarily a conciliation.[20]

The MRP had condemned the Third Republic and called itself the party of the Fourth Republic. But the political writer Raymond Aron referred to the MRP instead as the "Radical Socialists of the Fourth." He had told Maurice Schumann in 1948 that the party would have to choose between the "Fifth" and the Third; about two years later, on being asked by Aron what the choice was, Schumann replied that the MRP had chosen the Third. It was quite an achievement, said Aron sardonically in an interview with the author, to be able to change over to the "dirty political game of the Radicals" within five years.

The leaders of the MRP presumed to expel Denis and Hamon from the party for opposing its foreign policy, when they themselves, although to a lesser degree and more discreetly, disregarded or soft-pedaled it. But this is only one aspect of MRP dualism. The party Congresses, which in their resolutions endorsed MRP foreign policy in general and the policy of European integration in particular, gave as a rule only lip service to these policies. This study will reveal how little attention was devoted in the Congresses to foreign policy. The "European vocation" of the MRP, in particular, was preserved by relatively few of its leaders. In a way, this was proper retribution; the leaders had themselves brought on the situation by constructing such a centralized party.

It would not be too surprising to find that the party rank and file outside the Congresses gave scant heed to matters of foreign policy.

The main programs were developed (perhaps ratified is the better word) within, not outside, the official party gatherings of sections, federations, and National Congresses. Party policy was one thing and the attitude of the loyal electorate another. Voters for the MRP did not feel bound very much by its pronouncements; there was *un pays légal* and *un pays réel*. In 1951, a number of MRP militants (the most loyal adherents) were believed to have voted for the party program supporting NATO, although they were basically opposed to it. But even those who voted for the party did not necessarily feel *engagés*, although they had no alternative solution to NATO to offer.

It was, or should have been, even more disturbing for the party that at the organized meetings themselves there was relatively little enthusiasm for matters of foreign policy. Since 1950, European integration had been the focal point not only of MRP foreign policy but of its policy in general. Yet a careful examination of the proceedings of the meetings of the sections, federations, and National Congresses reveals that this program of integration, as well as foreign policy in general, usually took a back seat to matters of domestic politics. This is not unusual, of course, in any country and especially in France. When the critical issue of Indochina policy was raised, for example, in the Peasant Party Congress in the spring of 1953, the answer was, "No! No! No distractions!" Of all the parties, only the Socialists paid more attention to foreign policy in their party gatherings than did the MRP.[21] But the important thing is how little attention was paid to it in MRP gatherings, when the party sought by various devices to retain control of the foreign office for the primary purpose of preserving the continuity of its program of European integration.

The four main problems before the MRP Congress of 1950 were lodging, social security, full employment, and redistribution of national revenue. In the preliminary preparations for the Congress, no reference seems to have been made to foreign policy as such, although only three weeks previously, Schuman had made his sudden proposal for a Franco-German merger in coal and steel. Much attention was devoted to the family, and, in the federation meetings prior to the Congress, speakers had dwelt on internal affairs, such as the problem of rejuvenation of the French economy, with scant, if any, reference to the international factors involved. Domestic

problems were also stressed more than foreign problems in De
Menthon's leadership of the party in the National Assembly in
1950–51. Maurice Schumann, in his editorials in the party organ
L'Aube, had been dwelling on foreign affairs almost daily up until
about February, 1951. Then there was a strange and quite sudden
reversal as he directed his attention toward internal matters. Perhaps it was felt that this might boost a sagging circulation at a time
when the days of the journal seemed numbered. Perhaps it was in
preparation for the coming general elections. We do not know; but
if either of these suppositions is correct, it is another reflection of
the relative lack of interest of MRP adherents in foreign affairs.

At its Congress in Lyons in May, 1951, Goguel said that the
MRP had found again the "atmosphere of the party's birth." If so,
the original atmosphere of the party had little connection with
foreign policy, for no particular reference was made to foreign affairs, and the resolution on foreign policy was unusually vague. The
MRP was primarily concerned at this time with the imminent elections. In the political advertisements for this parliamentary election
of 1951, all parties except the Neutralists put their programs on
foreign policy in small print. The French actually voted on the
basis of internal policy, which gave a deceptive appearance to the
result as far as foreign policy was concerned.

On the other hand, at the Bordeaux MRP Congress of 1952,
coming as it did soon after the National Assembly debate on a European army and signing of the EDC Treaty, considerable attention
was devoted to foreign policy. The Congress formally expressed its
opposition to the revival of any German national army and demanded that the EDC Treaty be ratified only if it carried with it the
guarantees required by the National Assembly, in particular an effective guarantee from the United States and the United Kingdom
in the event of German secession. However, the party was in general
preoccupied with its attitude toward the Pinay Government, and
the debate on foreign policy, which was held on the last day of the
Congress when many had returned to their federations, seemed to
some of the militants to be more academic than those of former
years.

When the MRP National Committee met in January, 1953, internal policies did finally seem to yield first place to foreign policy,
and the same might be said in general for the discussions at the

Paris Congress of May, 1953. But the fate of the EDC was becoming more problematical with the passage of time, and the growth of interest within the body of the MRP had apparently come too late. During the spring of 1954, discussion in the early federation meetings was again devoted primarily to internal problems. For example, when the president of the strong Seine federation was empowered to make contacts to build a *majorité européenne et sociale,* there seemed to be more concern with building a political group that was well-knit on social questions than with finding a unified group on the European program. While there was greater attention to foreign affairs in the later federation meetings in May, 1954, still, certain leaders of the MRP were quite noncommittal when they took part in these meetings. There was no motion passed on foreign policy at the Bouches-du-Rhône meeting over which De Menthon presided, despite his own recent pronouncement of the need for action. In the resolutions at the meeting of the federation of Seine-Inférieure, presided over by Secretary-General Colin, there was no reference to the EDC. Although by this time almost half of the federations had taken a specific stand on the EDC Treaty, the above represent significant exceptions.

By the end of the party Congress at Lille in May, 1954, the MRP had taken the position that only a decision on the EDC would make possible the settlement of various internal problems. Yet the greater part of the attention of this Congress (which the author attended) still seemed to be devoted to domestic issues, which occupied the time of the delegates during Thursday, Friday, and part of Saturday. After two sessions devoted to foreign policy on Saturday afternoon and Sunday morning, the ticklish problems of the French Union and North Africa were handled rather summarily at the tag end of Sunday afternoon.

It is possible that the reason for the lack of attention to such matters as European integration and relations with the French Union and North Africa might have been found in the relative unanimity of the MRP on foreign policy. It must be admitted that this unanimity was a refreshing contrast to the dissension in the National Assembly, which had risen to a peak immediately prior to this Lille Congress. Nonetheless, there was also a striking contrast between the matter-of-fact acceptance of the MRP foreign-policy program and the great and exclusive attention given to foreign policy at the special Socialist convention called also in May, 1954, to reach a decision on the EDC. This relative disregard for foreign policy by the MRP, claiming as it did a unique "European vocation," seemed to be a reflection in miniature of what Luethy has referred to as the incredible indifference of the French people to foreign affairs.[22] Because of a lack of contacts with the French people other than those from limited geographic areas and because of particular religious inclinations, the MRP as a party was immobilized by its own centralized character to such an extent that it could not generate really active and continuous enthusiasm even within its own ranks for its program of European integration.[23]

3

Allies and Adversaries

By virtue of its name, the Mouvement Républicain Populaire had reason to extend its contacts and in so doing would be developing its mystique of pluralism. Not only was this necessary to gain support for a program of European integration, but it was in accord with the implications of another basic MRP doctrine, that peace is indivisible. For if peace is indivisible, then the interests of the nations of the world are indivisible, and, by the same token, the interests of potentially divisive groups within a nation are indivisible. The MRP would have done well to have attempted to develop this idea of a general interest. Why, for example, did it not do more to indicate the general value to consumers of the economic aspects of European integration? Certainly, as the Common Market has worked out, it has been much more to France's economic advantage than many had hoped it would be.

Of course, the MRP did develop this idea of the general interest indirectly in its propaganda for European integration. Also indirectly, the party did much to re-enforce France's European, if not world, position in its championing of the family. This most important natural group in society has experienced no less than a demographic revolution in France in the last fifteen years; and the increase in the fertility rate has done much to revive France and give it hope for the future. Politically, there is little doubt that the MRP has done more than any other party to build up the status of the family in France.

In agriculture, we see a different picture. Certainly the MRP drew much of its support from farmers in some regions, but they were conservative peasants rather than commercial farmers who might be more directly affected by the program of European integration. Its contacts with farmers were not nearly as great as those of the Communists, who developed quite a rural press. MRP party pronouncements, moreover, were frequently equivocal in relating problems of agriculture to the program of integration, and, as we shall see, there was little enthusiasm within the party for the plan of its own leader, Pflimlin, for a "green pool" for European agriculture.

As for the scientific and intellectual communities of France, it appears that MRP ideology, being humanistic rather than materialistic or scientific, had scant appeal for natural or physical scientists, and there is little contact between the party and this area of science. There is also a relative lack of support by the intellectuals in the social sciences (who are much more important in political life in France than in the United States), as well as a lack of effort on the part of the MRP to seek the support of intellectuals outside the party. Of course, we must identify Étienne Borne, and before him Gilson and Gortais, as intellectuals within the MRP. We must also note that François Goguel and, much more hesitantly, François Mauriac gave limited support from without. Moreover, perhaps the relation of intellectualism to French politics has been exaggerated; perhaps no particular French party has had as much intellectual support as, say, the Kennedy Democratic Administration in its first year in the United States.

For the rest of this chapter we shall be concerned with contacts made by the MRP with religious, economic, and journalistic groups. As the situation actually developed, the only really active allies of the MRP in its program of integration were to be found within Catholic groups. The party had very slim contacts with business, where there were many foes of integration, and sections of labor and of the press were increasingly alienated from the MRP. Finally, in some aspects of MRP foreign policy, the bureaucracy, an interest group in itself, tended to control rather than to support some of the party's leaders.

Religious Organizations and the European Movement

MRP leadership stressed the need for bringing the program of European integration to the attention of "every social and spiritual family." How they all might participate in the program was never made clear. As a matter of fact, some of the "spiritual families" that did participate most actively were already transnational in character. Moreover, one gets the impression, even without having sufficient statistics at hand to verify it completely, that there was considerable identity of personnel among these several organizations. All of this should not be too surprising. Hannah Arendt has indicated that it is not unusual for political groups that claim to be movements to remain in fact small societies of intellectuals (or interlocking directorates of quasi intellectuals).[1]

In actuality, then, the Christian-democratic approach in the MRP mystique of this European program was transformed into a social-Catholic implementation of it. The reader will remember the distinction between these two wings of Catholicism—the initiative proceding from the top down in social Catholicism, from the bottom up in Christian democracy.[2] In the former, there would be less support for direct representation of people of national groups in the legislative branches of European communities.

Included in the groups supporting the principle of European integration, although questioning certain applications of it, was the strong Association Catholique de la Jeunesse Française (ACJF), which from the beginning had been social Catholic rather than Christian democratic by inclination. This organization —whose federal council included representatives of the Jeunesse Agricole Chrétienne (JAC), Jeunesse Etudiante Chrétienne (JEC), Jeunesse Maritime Chrétienne (JMC), and Jeunesse Ouvrière Chrétienne (JOC)[3]—at first steered clear of parties, but by 1946 pushed its militants into active support of the MRP. At the same time as it supported integration of workers into international communities and improvement of legal forms permitting international organizations to be created, the ACJF looked askance at such a specific project as the European Defense Community, seeing in it a medium through which German industrial combines would be reconstituted. The fact that such MRP leaders as Teitgen and Colin had also been prominent members of the ACJF tended to put a damper on any enthusiasm they might have had for such projects as the EDC.

In addition to the participation of youth groups, the Catholic Church itself made a contribution to the program of European integration. Since the time of the Holy Roman Empire, the approach of Catholicism had been transnational rather than national. The Separation of 1905 in France had brought the Church closer both to the people and to Rome. As the movement for European integration began to gain momentum in June, 1950, French cardinals and archbishops made a declaration that a Christian (meaning a practicing Catholic) did not have the right to be uninterested in efforts to build a Europe. Two years later, the Pope put the Church officially behind the movement for integration, but pointed out that political ties alone were not enough to sustain the movement.[4]

Political ties had their value, however. Leaders of the Catholic parties of Europe had frequently consulted together in the past to harmonize their policies. There were also important personal contacts among leaders of the Christian-democratic parties. Schuman, while Minister of Foreign Affairs, was fortunate in having contacts through religion as well as through a common language (German) with the German and Italian political leaders Adenauer and De Gasperi. Teitgen also had direct contacts with the Christian Democratic Union in Germany, but, like Bidault, was more inclined to be distrustful of that nation.

There were various transnational organizations connected with the Church, and through it with the MRP, that supported the principle of European integration. In fact, it appeared that a new type of Catholic was emerging who favored participating in temporal tasks, such as that of integrating Europe, and who was at the same time turning away from *integrism* (the policy of seeking sufficiency within one's own religion), which had tended toward paralysis of the Church in Europe. Actively associated with these Catholic organizations were such MRP leaders as Millot, Bichet, Bacon, and Farine. Moreover, qualified but specific support for projects of European integration was continuously given by the influential Nouvelles Équipes Internationales, (NEI), which was the first European organization after 1945 that took the initiative to include Germans. Bichet, MRP member of the National Assembly, served as President of the NEI until 1949 and thereafter as Secretary-General.

Relations with Labor and Business

The social-Catholic or Rightist Catholic composition of most of the religious organizations supporting European integration contributed to an alienation from this program of a considerable portion of the Catholic labor force in France. The Confédération

Française des Travailleurs Chrétiens (CFTC), which had 900,000 members in 1948 including various leaders of the MRP, was frequently at odds with MRP leadership and by 1952 was becoming alienated from the Church as well. Hence, it was little inclined to follow the directives of Church leaders requiring support for European integration. It was on this very issue of integration that a split occurred in the ranks of the CFTC in 1954. The resulting Left-wing group was quite pointed in its criticism of various phases of integration, and even the Right wing refused to take a stand in support of the specific plan for a European Defense Community. Other Catholic workers' organizations, specifically the Mouvement de Libération du Peuple and the Mouvement de Libération Ouvrière, took similarly critical stands on particular phases of European integration.

At the same time as the MRP was attempting to rally the support of various Catholic groups, including labor groups, to the cause of integration, it was strangely unconcerned about its failure to establish adequate ties with the French business world and the bureaucracy, which were directly concerned respectively with the economic and the political aspects of integration.

Lack of business support for a party in France is not as unusual as it might be in the United States. As Pflimlin indicated to the author, it is a reflection of the intellectual approach to politics in Europe compared to the practical approach in the United States. It is probable that MRP party doctrine had an effect on this relation with the business world. According to this doctrine, impersonal economic problems are considered distinctly subordinate to the importance of human relations. The MRP does not support a policy of *laissez faire*, which is still essentially the policy of much of the French business world.

Moreover, French businesses often seek to insulate themselves against the natural consequences of such a *laissez faire* policy. Yet, in its foreign policy doctrine, the MRP stresses the need for economic progress as a reflection of the growth of economic and social democracy. French business groups are very frequently opposed to the increase in competition that results from efforts at international economic progress. Finally, although the MRP in its domestic policy has opposed the increase of bureaucracy and has favored the re-establishment of initiative among business executives, it seems that in practice the implementation of the MRP program of European integration would lead to a considerable extension of bureaucracy. French business executives have unpleasant memories of bureaucratic control during World War II.

The only postwar business group that the MRP leadership considers without question to be close to the party is of a social-Catholic tendency, specifically the Cercle du Patronat Chrétien. In contrast, some of the most influential French business organizations have been opposed to the MRP program of European integration. The Conseil National du Patronat Français has been "afraid of Europe" (in the words of a business specialist in the MRP leadership), and the Confédération Générale des Petites et Moyennes Entreprises is even more conservative, not wanting the modernization of industry that is likely to follow integration of Western Europe.[5]

Schuman had reassured members of the MRP that the European Coal and Steel Community would not be controlled by vested interests. This possibility was exactly what troubled many leaders of French industries. The French steel manufacturers were intensely annoyed at the Schuman Plan from the beginning, first, because they had not been consulted, and second, because many of them could only think of it in terms of a government cartel. It would seem that they projected their own cartel complex onto the framers of the ECSC. The chief manufacturers' association in France soon began to warn against leaving control in the hands of "technicians," and L'Usine Nouvelle published the complaint that nations in the Plan would have to adjust themselves to German conditions.[6] Attacks by industry on the Schuman Plan continued inside and outside the National Assembly from early 1951 to 1954.

The usual method of French pressure groups is not to oppose directly a government that seems to be infringing on its vested interest but to wait and oppose it on something else. Industrial leaders were charged by Pflimlin with having conducted a press campaign against his "green pool" for agriculture in order indirectly to undermine the Schuman Plan. Opposition to this Pflimlin Plan for integration of European agriculture was at times either contradictory or unwarranted. Some commercial interests feared the subordination of agriculture to a new bureaucracy at the same time as other industrial leaders opposed the special protection they thought farmers would get. Others attacked the anticipated "omnipotent" high authority, which was no part of Pflimlin's Plan.[7]

After World War II, part of the domestic policy of the MRP had been to oppose the increase of bureaucracy. However, the relation of the party to the powerful bureaucracy at the Ministry of Foreign Affairs (Quai d'Orsay) appeared at times to be one of subservience rather than of opposition. This was most evident in the development of MRP policy toward North Africa, but in the autumn of 1953, it was evident also in the quality of MRP support for European integration. When Bidault was on vacation from the post of foreign minister in September of that year, a substitute draft for the European Political Community, minimizing its supranational features and reasserting French sovereignty, had been prepared by permanent officials at the Quai d'Orsay. This "wrecking operation" failed, not through the efforts of the MRP leaders but through the action of non-MRP Frenay. Perhaps by chance, perhaps not, MRP leaders had nothing particular to say about this incident.

MRP Influence in the Press

If the ties of the MRP with labor and business groups were somewhat tenuous, they were as much so with the fourth estate, the press. Communist parties usually have the advantage of a good "communication system";[8] the same could not be said for the MRP during the years in which it was most actively seeking European integration. This was especially unfortunate for the MRP in view of its claim to be a movement, with the resultant need for extensive contacts with the molders of public opinion in French journalistic circles. The influential, independent *Le Monde*, for example, gradually moved away from support for the MRP-sponsored European Defense Community.

The newspapers at one time directly connected with the MRP included *La Vie Catholique*, *L'Aube* (edited by Bidault in the 1930's), and the organ of the party Secretariat, *Forces Nouvelles*, which still appeared biweekly in 1954. Other journals that had some affinity with the party before 1950 were *Carrefour*, *La Tribune Économique*, and *Témoignage Chrétien*, as well as the MRP-inspired review *Politique*, which survived until about 1948. *Té-*

moignage Chrétien was still close to the Left wing of the MRP in 1954, although its editors disclaimed allegiance to any party. Offsetting this last journal was *La Croix*, with Right-wing affiliation. This official organ of French Catholicism did not come out in support of the EDC until 1953, while the Left-wing Catholic newspapers *Témoignage Chrétien* and *Monde Ouvrier Chrétien* had been opposing it for some time.

The newspaper most directly connected with the MRP was *L'Aube*. After having strongly resisted the Nazis and Fascists in the 1930's under the editorship of Bidault, it dropped in circulation from 230,000 in 1946 to 45,000 in 1951 and discontinued publication in July of that year. The very important policy statements made by MRP leaders in this journal failed to have much effect because of its small circulation in the last years of its life.[9]

The Parisian circulation of the MRP-oriented press declined after 1950, but the party fared better in the provinces, being represented especially by *Ouest France* in Brittany and *Nord Éclair* at Lille. French peasant opinion has always had an important although indirect bearing on the shaping of French foreign policy, and there has been, at least in the past, a traditionally close identity between the peasantry and Catholicism. Any party, such as the MRP, that relies strongly upon both is affected sooner or later by their fundamental conservatism.

The strongest MRP newspaper is the provincial *Ouest France*, published in Rennes in Brittany. Its predecessor, the *Ouest Éclair*, was one of the earliest social-Catholic journals in the provinces. Henri Teitgen, father of the MRP perennial President, had become its editor in 1909. As early as 1910, after Sangnier's *Sillon* had been condemned by Pius X, *Ouest Éclair* slowly and prudently moved away from its former support for the Christian democrat Sangnier. Although the paper supported the Briand policy after World War I, it thereafter became "*poincariste* . . . ready to doze in a tranquil *bourgeoisisme*." As *Ouest France* has grown in strength, it has become more conservative and more nationalistic. It is strong financially and had grown in circulation to 516,000 by August, 1953. It had by far the largest circulation of any provincial newspaper, the next in line being *Le Progrès de Lyon* with 319,000 in 1954.

Otherwise, a general regression of the MRP press had set in by

1954. At the time of the expiration of *L'Aube* in 1951, critics were of the opinion that the newspaper had tied itself too closely to Government policy and that the militants of the MRP were undermining its influence in seeking to preserve their freedom of action against the party *dirigeants* in the Government coalition. After a detailed examination of *L'Aube*—for the year prior to its demise— the author would agree that the journal did appear to be quite uncritical of the Government, in contrast to other Parisian newspapers. It is especially fashionable in France to criticize the Government.

Unlike the Communists, the MRP has been weak in having no newspaper organ in close contact with the farmers. The short-lived MRP journal *Terre Humaine*, edited by Borne, had no connection with agriculture despite its name. First published in 1951, it met an untimely death in 1953 that was symptomatic of the trouble the French press was having. Prices had risen, the number of newspapers had doubled since 1944, and there was little advertising to provide a source of income. The "free press of the Liberation had succumbed to the implacable logic of profit-and-loss accounting."[10] By 1954, MRP influence in such centers of journalistic and intellectual activity as Paris was fast declining. The party was subjected to many attacks in the influential journal *Esprit*, whose acid-tongued editor, Domenach, charged the *Terre Humaine* staff with supporting too close contacts with "imperialist America." Even the MRP leaders appeared to give scant attention to this temporary journalistic organ of theirs.

Recently, there has been some revival of MRP participation in the press. At least, party members are directly connected with the review *France Forum*, a magazine of political opinion, which includes among other contributions articles by MRP *dirigeants*. There is also a primarily intraparty periodical, *Action Civique et Politique*.

One way to make up for this decreased influence in the realm of ideas as reflected through the press might have been for the party to carry on an active campaign to develop on the local level a politically energetic citizenry that would be sympathetic to the party program. This would have been in line with the MRP's claim to be a movement. But by 1954, in the opinion of Francisque Gay, one of the greatest weaknesses of the party was its failure to maintain direct contacts with public opinion and to stress the "civic spirit."

At one point, it is true, the MRP leaders apparently attempted to extend their contacts with public opinion through the press. In 1951, party leaders in the Government sought to gain control of the influential and relatively independent Parisian journal *Le Monde*. In August of that year, Beuve-Méry had resigned as its editor, and he was replaced for a time by the MRP deputy Dupraz, Catrice of the staff of the defunct *L'Aube*, and others. Charges were advanced by the hypercritical Domenach that the removal of Beuve-Méry was an example of Government pressure instigated by the MRP. "The 'domestication' of *Le Monde* by MRP politicians supported by the money powers is in the political, national, and moral order a sinister development which measures the extent of a decadence," he said. This development seemed to demonstrate an unsuccessful attempt by the restricted MRP leadership to extend its contacts with public opinion as well as with party militants through the medium of the popular *Le Monde*. Critics among the MRP militants had found that before its demise the party organ *L'Aube* had been tying itself too closely to government policy.[11]

In order for the MRP to accomplish its purpose in a foreign policy as dynamic as its plan for European integration, as delicate as the problem of relation with Russia and the United States, and as difficult as its policy toward the French Union and North Africa, the party needed many supporters. It is true that the MRP was at the center of a series of active groups in the Catholic orbit. But besides having the disadvantages of being a regional party, it lacked proper contacts with business and was progressively losing contact with labor and the press during the period under consideration.

It should be said of the MRP, however, that these were handicaps rather than discredits. Despite the 1951 *Le Monde* incident, the MRP seemed generally clear of the venal connections with the press that were typical of some other French political parties. And, except for aspects of the North African affair, the slim contacts of the MRP with business meant that the party was not willing to cater to the special interests of this segment of French society at the expense of its long-term program of European integration.[12]

PART TWO

4

European Integration

Four Plans of Integration

Between 1950 and 1954, four plans were either sponsored or developed by the MRP in its program of European integration: the Schuman Plan, materializing in the European Coal and Steel Community; the Pleven Plan, which led to a draft treaty for a European Defense Community; the plan for a European Political Community; and the Pflimlin Plan for a "green pool" of European agricultural markets. Only the first, the ECSC, has so far been put into effect. (The surprisingly successful European Economic Community—the Common Market—based upon the Dutch Stikker Plan but inspired by the Schuman Plan, will be discussed below.) It is problematical how familiar even the most enthusiastic supporters of integration were with the details of these plans. Nevertheless, the MRP was committed to the principle of European integration and to a greater or lesser degree to each of the plans above. Hence, it is necessary to be familiar to some extent with the structures contemplated by these plans.

1. THE EUROPEAN COAL AND STEEL COMMUNITY. A fifty-year treaty providing for a European Coal and Steel Community was signed on April 18, 1951, and was ratified by the last of the six members (France, the German Federal Republic, Italy, Belgium, The Netherlands, and Luxembourg) in June, 1952. Five separate agencies are provided for—a High Authority, a Common Assembly, a Council of Ministers, a Court of Justice, and a Consultative Committee. The nine members of the High Authority are chosen directly or indirectly by the Council of Ministers and serve for six years. Actions of the Authority are taken by majority vote, and its functions include issuing directives to firms in the Community, securing access to their records, initiating borrowing and lending in

47

the name of the Community, exacting punishments and fines for violations of its rules, and raising taxes.

The legislative branch includes the Common Assembly and the Council of Ministers. The former was originally composed of seventy-eight members, with equal representation from France, West Germany, and Italy. Representatives are named by the respective parliaments of the member states and meet in Luxembourg. The Assembly may, by a two-thirds vote, censure the Authority or compel it to resign. Recommendations of the Authority must be approved by at least a five-sixths vote of the Council of Ministers, who must concur especially for the granting of loans or the admission of a new industry to the area. The Council generally acts by a majority vote, qualified by the provision that the majority must include either France or Germany. If there is a tie vote with France and Germany on opposite sides, the side including Germany is to prevail.

The Court of Justice is given the right to nullify the decisions of the Authority, the Assembly, and the Council. Appeals may also be taken to the Court on the basis of errors of omission of the Authority. The seven members of the Court are appointed to a six-year term by agreement of the member governments. All of the judgments of the Court are executory, requiring for their effect further action of member governments.

The Consultative Committee is advisory in capacity and represents in equal numbers three economic groups: producers, labor, and consumers.

The principles of the treaty (which applies specifically only to the European territories of its members) involve the development of a common market in coal and steel to reduce costs to producer and consumer and the elimination of restrictive practices, which can lead to the closing of the most inefficient plants. The High Authority has power to provide new investment, and it must help in the readjustment of workers who have been affected adversely by competition. It must approve mergers, can act to prevent dumping, and can exert price controls in periods of "manifest crisis," setting maximum prices and consumption priorities in periods of shortage or production quotas in periods of surplus. It cannot, however, actually close mines nor compel investments.

Transition periods are provided for the purpose of gradually eliminating tariff restrictions and equalizing cost conditions in the member countries.[1]

2. THE EUROPEAN DEFENSE COMMUNITY. On May 27, 1952, the same six nations that are members of the ECSC signed the European Defense Community Treaty. The Treaty, also of fifty years' duration, contemplated a common procurement of supplies by EDC authorities and a common military command by the SHAPE officials of NATO. National units were to be no larger than divisions. Until the formation of a European army was accomplished, voting was to be equal among France, West Germany, and Italy, which together had over three-fifths of all votes.

Four agencies were to be created by the Treaty: a Commissariat, an Assembly, a Council, and a Court of Justice. The Commissariat of nine members with a six-year tenure would handle administration, but would also be a supranational authority acting by majority vote and controlling all military appointments above the rank of national unit commanders.

The Assembly was to be the same as that of the ECSC, with the addition of three more representatives from each of the three larger states. It could, by a two-thirds vote, discharge the Commissariat. The Council—composed of one governmental representative of each member state—was to issue directives to the Commissariat. In case of a tie vote, a provision was made that the side that represented two-thirds of the total contributions to the common budget would win. The Court of Justice was to be the same as that under the ECSC.

This defensive Treaty provided for the stationing of forces in the "territories in Europe that lie within the region defined in Article 6 of the North Atlantic Treaty." NATO gave the embryonic EDC a guarantee that an armed attack on a member of the EDC, or in the area covered by Article 6 of the North Atlantic Treaty, would automatically call into effect Article 5 of the latter. The Senate of the United States ratified this in July, 1952. In addition, the United Kingdom gave the EDC a separate guarantee that while it was a member of NATO it would support the European Defense Community under the provisions of Article 51 of the United Nations Charter.

The military provisions of the Treaty contemplated a total force

of fifty-five divisions at the end of three years. Of the standing
forty divisions, France was to have fourteen, West Germany
twelve, and Italy eleven.[2]

3. THE EUROPEAN POLITICAL COMMUNITY. Article 38 of the
European Defense Community Treaty provided that at the end
of six months (after ratification) the EDC Assembly should make
specific proposals for a European Political Authority with a permanent democratically elected Assembly, whose main function
would be to coordinate defense policy. During the autumn and
winter of 1952–53, a twenty-six-member preconstituent-committee
was engaged in drafting a charter for a European Political Community and the basic plan was ready by March.

All the territory belonging to the six nations that were to be
members of the EDC was to come under the jurisdiction of the
"European Community" unless exemptions were declared at the
time of ratification. The legislature was to be composed of two
houses with five-year terms, the lower chamber to be chosen by
direct election, employing proportional representation. France
was to have the maximum number of seats for any member,
seventy, and Italy and West Germany were to follow with sixty-
three each. The Senate would be composed of the national members of the six states in the Consultative Assembly of the Council
of Europe, would have a veto power, and also would elect, by
absolute majority vote, the "President of Europe." In turn he
would choose a six-member cabinet, subject to the approval of
both houses, and, sitting with this cabinet or council, would be
the President of the High Authority of the ECSC and the Chairman of the EDC Commissariat.

Wide powers were provided for the Community in the field
of foreign affairs with respect to the appointment of diplomatic
representatives and negotiation with nonmembers and with other
international organizations. A special protocol provided for an
annual report to the Council of Europe. In addition, provision
was made for the gradual removal of economic barriers. For the
first year of its existence, no initiative would reside in the European
Community, but in the following five years, barriers could be removed by unanimous consent of the Committee of National Ministers, which was to be an adjunct of the Community, and sub-

sequently by their majority vote plus a two-thirds vote of both houses of the legislature.

4. THE PFLIMLIN PLAN. The Pflimlin Plan existed in a state of suspended animation for several years without ever taking definitive form. In June, 1950, Pierre Pflimlin suggested a European agricultural pool. Early in 1951, under the sponsorship of the Council of Europe, a conference was held on this proposal in Paris. Not much was accomplished, partly, from the French standpoint, because of rising concern over how it would affect the farm-subsidy system.

In March, 1952, another "Preparatory Conference on the Organization of European Agricultural Markets" was attended by sixteen European states to consider two proposals—that of Pflimlin and a Dutch proposal. The former—the French Government plan put into a somewhat definitive shape by Pflimlin in May, 1951—contrasted with the Dutch plan in that it limited agricultural integration to four commodities (wheat, wine, sugar, and dairy products) and made the reduction of economic barriers subject to equalization of cost conditions in the various countries. The Dutch proposal would have had reduction and equalization go hand in hand. The objectives of both were to raise the standard of living, lower prices to consumers, eliminate barriers to trade, and expand specialized production. Pflimlin based his plan on the argument that a European organization of agriculture would support a modernization program for industry by establishing confidence in a continuing foreign market.

The Conference of March, 1952, approved the ideas implicit in the French and Dutch plans and created a working party to prepare for a conference in the autumn to determine the constitution and powers of such a community as these ideas would necessitate. One problem was whether such a community would have supranational features. The previous year, Charpentier of the MRP had presented a rather complete project to the Consultative Assembly of the Council of Europe at Strasbourg. It was similar to the Pflimlin Plan but went beyond it to provide for a "high authority" such as that in the ECSC. In 1954, in commenting on the failure of the governments concerned to take any further positive steps toward an agricultural pool, Pflimlin suggested to the author that opponents may have confused the Charpentier plan with his, which, he said, contained no such supranational features.

MRP Support for Integration

The principal purpose of the MRP program of European integration was to solve the difficult German problem. The party sought to convince France in particular and Western Europe in general that a greater security could be achieved through the construction of a "Europe." In this way, the party related its program of integration to what had at times approximated an almost pathological French search for security. In supporting the Schuman Plan, the MRP emphasized that two objectives would be achieved, one political and one economic. Europe would be freed of the old feud between France and Germany. At the same time, the incrustations on France's national economy would be sloughed off, and the level of living would be raised in France as well as elsewhere.

Prior to the announcement of the Schuman Plan of 1950, a new attitude toward Germany was actually quite slow in developing even within the MRP. At its Congress of 1945, emphasis was placed on the need for keeping Germany strictly within bounds. Even in early 1950, many MRP leaders seemed to desire no closer accord with Germany than France had with other countries of Europe. The "Atlantic High Council" proposed by Bidault at this time was to be open to all European countries, including Russia. Its purpose was apparently to provide a frame into which West Germany could be brought without admitting her directly to NATO. In 1948, Robert Schuman had come closer to a new approach to the German problem when he declared that the Ruhr problem must be solved on a European basis. It was he who seized the initiative as French Minister of Foreign Affairs in May, 1950, when he proposed an economic union between France and Germany in the production and distribution of the two basic commodities, coal and steel.

The suddenness of this step provided France with a tactical advantage. The objective was also quite practical and realistic in contrast to the vagueness of many MRP programs, although such vagueness is typical of parties in France. If the choice of coal and steel seemed an arbitrary starting point for European integration, it must be remembered that the demand for steel is tied to invest-ment policies, and the latter in turn have a psychological effect on the relative optimism of business. French business needed a boost, which was unlikely to come from any program of national economic integration within France alone, since in the past consolidation of business in France had tended to protect inefficient units against competition rather than lead to greater efficiency.

Difficulties were, of course, involved in getting support for the Schuman Plan. The very possibility that more efficiency might result from the Schuman Plan was partly responsible for the oppo-sition to it. De Gaulle, for example, opposed any organization composed of what he called "technocrats."[3] Yet, one of the pri-mary purposes of the Schuman Plan had been to create an organi-zation that would be independent of French business groups or, rather, would represent equally the interests of employers, em-ployees, and consumers. Schuman had reassured the delegates to the MRP Congress of 1950 on the matter of control of the new high authority by vested interests.

When in turn the Pleven Plan for a European army came up for discussion, difficulties were immediately foreseen by various MRP leaders. In a National Committee meeting in October, 1950, Scherer referred to the legal problem of rearming a country still technically an enemy. Henri Meck, member of the MRP group in the National Assembly, argued that atomic power had trans-formed the whole nature of the German problem. There was also some confusion about the distinction between demilitarization and neutralization of Germany, as possible alternatives to re-armament.

Although one characteristic of a movement is the presence of a small directorate but the relative absence of individual stars,[4] this was not true of the MRP, at least in respect to its program of European integration. Perhaps in its domestic policy there were no particularly outstanding leaders, but individuals were closely as-sociated with most of the phases of integration. Schuman was the sponsor of the ECSC,[5] Pflimlin of the "green pool," and Teitgen was the most enthusiastic backer of the EPC. As an ex-ception, no one in the MRP was particularly eager to become identified with the European Defense Community.

Robert Schuman is a special case. A devout Catholic and a

bachelor, he is the most religious man in a religious party. Born in
Lorraine, he had not become French until the time of the Treaty
of Versailles. Schuman had one "passionate dream," which was to
end the Franco-German feud. In a tribute in 1950 to Bech, Foreign
Minister of Luxembourg, he said that "we people of the frontiers"
were predestined to understand and resolve international problems. As an idealist, Schuman discounted party or class considerations in his search for Franco-German understanding. Although
some found "nothing of the revolutionary about this dry, phleg-
matic lawyer from Lorraine," an opponent said of him during a debate on the Schuman Plan in the National Assembly, "The greatest revolutionaries are the soft-spoken ones."[6]

The seasoned political observer Raymond Aron made the somewhat harsh observation that the whole European policy of the
MRP was an accident. This seems to be inaccurate at least with
respect to the Schuman Plan. We have seen that the MRP had
been considering some such step for a long time. The situation
was different, however, in the case of the proposal for a European
Defense Community. Here, perhaps, MRP support for the plan
might be said to have originated in an accident. The party as a
whole regretted that the issue had been raised, at least as early
as 1950. Schuman declared later, in June, 1952, that it was wrong to
believe that the EDC was an "essential of European integration."
It was rather to have been the final stage, but had been supported
sooner than desired by the MRP.

Even in the case of the EDC, however, certain MRP leaders
had had a hand in the preliminaries. As early as August, 1950,
Teitgen and Bidault had suggested steps toward a common defense of Western Europe, and Schuman had stood alone in September against the proposal by other NATO Council members
for German national rearmament.

It was at this time, in September, 1950, that General de Gaulle
had become the catalytic agent for the development of a European
Political Community when he asked, "How can one seriously con-
ceive of a European army when Europe does not exist?"[7] MRP
leaders conceded that the adoption of the EDC alone would have
put the cart before the horse. Hence, if the EDC was an accident
in MRP foreign policy, so was the EPC. And prior to the autumn
of 1952, party leaders were in no particular hurry to create such a
political community.

One other project in the program of European integration, the Pflimlin Plan, is even more clearly identified with the MRP leadership than the Schuman Plan. Schuman is from Lorraine; the originator of the "green pool" for agriculture, Pierre Pflimlin, is from neighboring Alsace. The fact that Pflimlin had been Minister of Agriculture between 1947 and 1951 had given him a chance to become familiar with the subject. In 1947, referring to France's status as an international debtor, he argued that a European plan should be quickly drafted to create a favorable climate for exporters (but the unfavorable climate for French exporters was very much the result of French quotas and tariff walls).

This European plan for an agricultural pool was not quickly drafted; in fact, we have seen how it petered out after having been considered in two conferences by sixteen European states. At the MRP Congress of 1954, it was Pflimlin who recalled the attention of the delegates to the economic phase of the construction of Europe, especially to his "green pool." Not only had the party recently given scant attention to the Pflimlin Plan, but it had also begun to soft-pedal proposals within the MRP for support of the Dutch Stikker Plan for a common European market. As early as July, 1950, Schuman had declared that this Stikker Plan would not conflict with the Schuman Plan. But throughout the years up to 1954, reference in MRP circles to a scheme for a common market was conspicuous by its absence.

There may be two reasons for this. First, it is to be remembered that the Pflimlin Plan was diametrically opposed to the Dutch Plan in contemplating integration of only a few agricultural commodities and in favoring reduction of trade barriers only after costs had been equalized internationally. (Are they ever?) Secondly, the plan for an EPC included provision for gradual movement toward a common market; perhaps MRP leaders were reluctant to see it developed outside the sheltering wings of that community.

Pluralism in European Integration

In its leadership of a congeries of groups in the European movement, the MRP applied, consciously or unconsciously, its own doctrine of pluralism, however imperfectly MRP leaders may have agreed upon its definition.[8] One of the most internationally minded of these groups, the NEI, explicitly pronounced itself in favor of pluralism in every domain. Bidault declared in 1951 that there is a need for defense against the growth of international monism, which would lead to the concentration of power within a single group.[9] But the European movement with which the MRP was so closely connected was limited in any efforts to develop pluralism by the inadequate contacts of the MRP with business, labor, and intellectuals. As one examines the leadership of the various Catholic or quasi-Catholic groups involved in this movement, one is struck by the recurrence of the same relatively few individuals in positions of importance. Hence, the breadth of influence essential for effective operation of the European movement was limited by an interlocking-directorate type of control, especially since there was no outstanding leader among the group of interlocking directors, at least in the MRP-oriented fraction of this movement.

To the extent that pluralism was not reflected in the MRP program of European integration, party practice was inconsistent with party doctrine. On the other hand, to the extent that pluralism was present, it provided a particular obstacle to successful development of the program. For pluralism attacks the sovereignty of the state in the process of obliterating its uniqueness among human associations. The idea of sovereignty had been developed by the Frenchman Bodin; sovereignty had reached its zenith under the Sun King, Louis XIV. Time after time in debates on European integration, members of the National Assembly were admonished to protect French sovereignty. Charges of treason were leveled against MRP sponsors of the supranational communities that were being considered. This was especially true in the case of the EDC, whose supranational features have been summarized above. In the debate of November, 1953, one speaker in the National Assembly told his audience, "You are French in all the fibers of your being; protect your nationality!" In August, 1954, the "grand old man" Herriot was one of only two speakers allowed before a final vote on the EDC. "On the threshold of death," he said, "let me tell you that EDC is the end of France."[10]

In an attempt to counteract this kind of attack, MRP leaders reminded their hearers in the National Assembly of the party's record in the Resistance. The party President, Teitgen, in February, 1952, also argued that France's mission had always been to undertake "crusades"; her mission today was to make a Europe. Bidault declared, in the same National Assembly debate, that France was in line with her oldest tradition in supporting a European Defense Community. There are three things for which men die, he said: a *coin de terre* (piece of land), their nation, and an idea.[11] By his order of priority, Bidault demonstrated that nationalism was above other considerations in his own mind.

In France, the state in its growth has tended to choke off rivals for power such as the Church. It could be that the MRP adopted pluralism with the underlying, if unconscious, purpose of counteracting this tendency in the interests of the Church. It was relatively easy for the party to sponsor pluralism in the program of European integration because of its close contacts with the transnational community of the Catholic Church. But the narrowness of MRP group contacts on the domestic scene aggravated its difficulties in trying to develop this program.

Functionalism

Although MRP leaders did not directly connect the party doctrine of pluralism with the program of integration, pluralistic qualities were to be found in the functionalism implicit in three of the four plans in the program. There was emphasis on functionalism in the Schuman Plan, which materialized into the ECSC. For functionalism involves the creation of a new and separate center of control over a particular field of economic, political, or social activity. It is the functional approach to set up some such high authority as was provided for in the ECSC, which is not subordinate to the sovereignty of any particular state and is oriented toward the performance of a particular political, economic, or military task. A prime objective of functionalism in the international field, as also of pluralism, is to cut down the centralized control of states.

The Pleven Plan for an EDC had been an expression of functionalism in that it contemplated only the creation of a common army with suitable consultative machinery or controls, such as a legislative body. But this necessitated a common foreign policy, and eventually a provision was incorporated in the EDC Treaty, which had been drafted under the guidance of Schuman, to the effect that, within six months of ratification, steps were to be taken to create a political community.

At first, it seems difficult to detect functionalism, and therefore pluralism, in the MRP project for a European Political Community. If a common European foreign policy was the goal of the EPC, the project seemed to be closer to federalism, with its division of power in the broader sense among different levels of government. Moreover, if a common European foreign policy was supposed to be created through such an organization, this development would seem to lead toward monism with its centralization of power, rather than toward pluralism. As far as party doctrine is concerned, the MRP would appear to have been contradicting itself in its support for the EPC. However, MRP leaders sought in some instances to eliminate a common foreign policy from the jurisdiction of an EPC, thus minimizing the monistic aspects of this plan and bringing it closer to the functional approach. In fact, Pflimlin argued that a common foreign policy could not exist in an organization where some, but not all, of the member nations had unsatisfied territorial claims. Therefore, he contended that the EPC would be neither federation nor confederation, since both of these required a common foreign policy.[12]

The multiplicity of integration plans, one coming on the heels of another, created in itself an obstacle for the MRP. Instead of providing for "too little, too late," the party subjected itself to the charge of seeking "too much, too soon." Especially in a unitary state like France, where there is distaste for any quasi-federalistic arrangement, if the MRP had confined itself to more practical functional plans, in the proper sense, such as those of Schuman and Pflimlin (and Stikker), the party might have been more successful in the long run. Less than three years after the MRP Congress of 1954, six Western European governments, including that of France, agreed on a Common Market and also on an Atomic Energy Community. The structure of these two new communities was patterned to a great extent upon that of the MRP-sponsored ECSC, which the former was eventually to absorb.

Strategic Retreats

MRP doctrine as reflected in party publications made much of the disregard by the party for electoral success or failure in the

process of sponsoring certain "values" in politics. It was the belief
of party leaders that some of these values were to be achieved
through the program of integration. But these leaders had continuously to conciliate other political groups within France in
order to participate in the Government and thereby to maintain
the continuity of this program. This participation of the MRP in
the political leadership of France between 1944 and 1954 was quite
unusual. Credit for holding the greatest number of government
posts under the fourteen relatively permanent governments that
existed between 1946 and 1953 goes to Schuman (twelve), Bidault
(eight), and Buron (seven). Furthermore, for the ten years from
1944 to 1954, with the exception of one month, a member of the
MRP was in charge of the foreign office.

Not only did MRP leaders conciliate other groups in domestic
policy in order to achieve their goal of integration, but they themselves had to compromise in this area of their foreign policy. In
fact, the support for the European Defense Community in itself
represented such a compromise. The Pleven Plan of October, 1950,
for such a community had been devised as an alternative to the
German national rearmament that had been supported at the recent NATO Council meeting by all participants except French
Minister of Foreign Affairs Schuman. Many members of the MRP
disliked this plan for a military community and did not agree with
President Teitgen when he argued that the creation of an EDC
would be a continuation of a Leftist policy. It appeared to them
that the party was being forced continually closer to the political
Right in France.[13] In turn, the European Political Community represented a compromise by MRP leaders, since to many of them
it was an unwanted child of the EDC, a result of the illogical attempt to create a common army in the absence of any machinery
for a common foreign policy for Western Europe.

It is striking to observe the transition from the unusual willingness of some of the MRP leaders to compromise, in the earlier
stages of the program of European integration, to a peculiar degree
of inflexibility in the later stages, especially after the early part
of 1954.[14] In general, though, there appeared to be a doctrinal preference by MRP leaders for conciliation rather than compromise.
In other words, rather than give in on certain points, they were
inclined to hold back, to procrastinate, to bide their time until the
mood of others had changed, so that the party might achieve its

original purpose. Although, in a series of coalition governments, the patience and tenacity of this self-styled "party of tomorrow" reflected its desire to conciliate, it also resulted in a degree of tolerance that was unusual even in the realm of politics and probably unwise from the party's standpoint because of the effect upon its own foreign policy program.

Obstacles to Integration

In the context of contemporary European politics and power relations, the MRP objective of European integration was quite realistic. Such a conclusion presupposes, however, some agreement that even in power politics there is a certain "safety in numbers." In other words, a balance of power is more precarious when it is confined to a balance between only two large powers, such as the United States and Russia. If Western Europe could develop into a third power through integration, then it might exert a moderating influence on the other two. This is the meaning of the statement that the MRP policy of integration was realistic, and increasingly it appears to be so.

Despite the failure of three of the four MRP-sponsored plans, at least the idea of integration was preserved through the ECSC, until such time as plans like Euratom and the European Common Market could materialize. Perhaps the idea of integration was as potent as the fact of further integration might have been. For one thing, the project for a European Defense Community pushed Russia and the three Western powers together, at least to the extent of carrying on extensive negotiations in 1954.

At least some of the MRP plans for integration appear to have been adopted by accident, or else as an escape from difficulties existing within France.[15] Moreover, politicians might well have been the most ardent supporters of the "construction of Europe," since the resultant development of an international bureaucracy and international legislatures would have provided them with additional employment. But whatever the motives, or whatever the origin of the program of integration, members of the MRP were very closely connected with it, at least until 1954.

The MRP certainly had to meet considerable opposition in supporting its program of integration. Under the impression that it had been by-passed on the European Coal and Steel Community, the steel industry in general opposed the European Defense Community. Besides the business groups, there were other opponents, such as the National Committee for the Defense of France and the French Union, which included two hundred members of the French parliament, and the International Conference of Countries Concerned in the European Defense Community. The tactics of the latter were illustrated by their "one belief" in common: Anything is better than war; the EDC would lead to war; hence, anything is better than the EDC.[16] In a way, the opposition of such groups was an indirect compliment to the MRP, in view of the party's economic and political objectives in the program of integration.

No particular constitutional obstacle stood in the way of the MRP program.[17] But there were many other difficulties. Some of these were found in the haste to build a bulwark against Communism, the fear of a resurgent Germany, and the uncertainties as to what type of Europe and how large a Europe should be built. Some MRP leaders recognized that considerable time was needed to revamp a French foreign policy that prior to 1940 had been oriented around preservation of the *status quo*. Unfortunately, time was not running in favor of the MRP.

One of the main reasons for the party's program of European integration was the need to enfold a dangerous Germany within some sort of European framework. Germany had always needed a "myth," said Teitgen to the MRP Congress of 1953; give her one, therefore, in that of Europe. But the myth of German unity was at the time gradually replacing the myth of Europe in the minds of many Germans.[18]

The fear of Germany permeated many political groups in France, including the MRP itself. Nonetheless, a party poll taken in June, 1953, indicated that, of those members questioned, 23 per cent chose Russia as France's chief enemy, and only 17 per cent chose Germany. MRP leaders developed elaborate arguments in party periodicals to demonstrate how much less dangerous Germany would be if incorporated in a European community. But these arguments did not reach enough people. Party leaders in parliament did not speak up clearly nor frequently enough to overcome fears engendered by the frequent warnings against Germany of other political leaders. Elderly MRP leaders like Schuman and Poher were aware of the dangerous parallel between the development in Franco-German relations after 1945 and that of the 1920's, when French opposition to Germany stimulated a revival of German militarism in the 1930's. But even within party circles they did not present this lesson of history frequently enough to the attention of younger members of the party.

As important as the haste and the fears was the uncertainty within the MRP over what kind of Europe should be constructed. Was it to be one of six nations or of more, one including England or not, one with general powers in the field of foreign policy or with only specific functions, and if the latter, which ones? Europe meant different things to different people. In fact, in his journals written soon after the end of World War II, Mauriac, who was at one time a member of the MRP, reminded his readers that the Germans had distorted for the French the idea of Europe. "When a Frenchman said, 'Before everything, I am a European,' we knew that it meant, 'I have chosen to be a traitor.' "[19]

An especially difficult problem for the party was whether England should be counted as part of this Europe. Maurice Schumann, troubled by England's refusal to join France in developing the Schuman Plan, commented that one wonders sometime whether England is European. The only way to find out, he concluded, was to *make* a Europe. Bidault told the National Assembly in November, 1950, that they could not wait forever for the British. The latter might follow afterward; it was France's experience, said Bidault, that the British are "the . . . readiest to assume responsibilities that are not theirs." The Labour Government in Great Britain had been concerned about the lack of socialist representation in the drafting of the Schuman Plan. If there were an attempt, said Bidault, to make a socialist Europe, a liberal Europe, or a Christian-democratic Europe, there would never be one. "Let us advance," he concluded, "with those who choose to follow us."[20]

Of course, Christian democrats would be clearly in a minority in a Europe that included either England or the Scandinavian states. But even if this had been a consideration, definite handicaps existed in disregarding Great Britain while creating a Europe of Six, such as was found in the ECSC. Without Great Britain, said De Menthon, a Europe of Six would not only run the risk of

German hegemony but also would be relatively weak in controlling supplies of raw materials from overseas territories. Although MRP leaders were agreed that they must start with a Europe of Six, Teitgen and De Menthon in particular supported the Eden Plan providing for close ties between England and the Council of Europe, which in turn was to be linked with the Six. With respect to Eden's appeal that the fullest use be made of existing institutions, Schuman said, "What a typical British anxiety, and how I wish it were more often a French anxiety!"[21]

Within France, the MRP leadership had to seek ways of reconciling the pluralistic implications of the program of European integration with the demands of the stanch defenders of French sovereignty. In November, 1953, for example, Bidault argued equivocally that a new formula must be found for the European Political Community, providing for "sovereign states exercising supranational functions." Thus, he saw the EPC as expressing some sort of combination of functionalism and nationalism; in fact, at this time he specifically rejected the interpretation of the EPC as either a federation or confederation.[22]

Besides being very cautious about injuring French sensibilities on the question of sovereign rights, the MRP had to be very careful about prospective relations between the European Political Community and the French Union. Should the French Republic (the French Union minus Indochina) be admitted to the EPC in its entirety? Teitgen alleged that this would prevent a split in French overseas territories, which was being fostered by Anglo-Saxon propaganda for a "United States of Africa." The final draft of the EPC treaty provided that the French Republic itself could arrange for the progressive participation of its component parts in the EPC.[23]

France is caught paradoxically between nostalgia for the past and a search for new solutions. During the debate on foreign policy at the MRP Congress of 1950, Bidault struck a typically French note when he said, "There is something against which one is never right . . . the nation." Hourdin of the MRP commented elsewhere that, although a Frenchman refuses to accept the idea of "My country, right or wrong," in internal affairs, the idea was doubtless well accepted as to "exteriors."[24]

The MRP took its most nationalistic stand toward the troublesome Saar problem. In 1952, Schuman had told the executive body of the ECSC that "of course the French will never accept a pure and simple return of the Saar to Germany." In his bid for the premiership in June, 1953, Bidault made prior agreement on the status of the Saar a condition for the settlement of the EDC issue. Not until the Lille Congress of 1954 did Schuman criticize the "sabotage" that had been carried on by permanent officials of the Quai d'Orsay to prevent any alteration of the status of the Saar.[25] It was typical of the MRP leadership not to attack such demonstrations of nationalism until well after the event, if at all.

It is quite evident that there was a clash between the emphasis in MRP doctrine on pluralism and a pluralistic internationalism and the nationalistic attitudes of certain members of the MRP leadership. The doctrinal approach may have been the result of the close contacts of the MRP with the transnational community of the Catholic Church. The "blind spots" of some leaders, such as Schuman, on the issue of the preservation of sovereignty with respect to the program of integration were partly due to the fact that they were in closer contact with this community than other leaders were. They were also partly due to the earnestness of these leaders. For them, at least, integration was no "escape into Europe" but an attempt at a positive and constructive solution of existing problems, especially that of Germany. And in retrospect, the arguments of MRP leaders in support of this program have become increasingly impressive.[26]

5

The MRP and the Cold War

Besides its objective of European integration, a second principal aim of the MRP was to maintain continuous contact between Russia and the West. According to party doctrine, France's proper role was that of mediator between the two blocs; merely to be against Communism was too negative a stand. In the process of maintaining a bridge between East and West, the MRP leaders refused to dramatize disturbing incidents and sought to be patient but to negotiate with either side from a position of strength. Negotiations with China also were favored, on the theory that this would keep Russia and China farther apart.

Its ideological opposition to blocs brought the MRP close to the position of the neutralists, in some respects. In fact, prior to 1951, an influential member of the MRP was a leader of the neutralists. Yet the MRP leadership found it necessary to disavow neutralism, especially because of its damaging effect on the program of European integration.

Despite the hints of neutralism in party ideology and personal ties with the neutralists, the MRP was such a consistent supporter of United States foreign policy that it was called the "American party" in France. Actually, it maintained at the same time quite an independent and critical position toward the tenor of American policy. It especially opposed the idea of a "roll-back" policy or a "crusade" against Russia. At the same time, however, the leaders of the MRP were philosophically opposed to compromises by France itself with the Communist powers. For example, bargains were not to be made with them in Asia to facilitate the program of European integration. Strictly speaking, it was the policy of the party to conciliate (mollify, gain, win) rather than to compromise (make a settlement by concessions). The MRP leaders, guided by the belief that one compromise inevitably led to others, sought to reduce friction between East and West and await the moment when the party's foreign policies might more easily be achieved.

The MRP Seeks a Middle Way

In classifying French parties, one is justified in placing the MRP apart from the Radical Socialists and the Communists rather than between them. For MRP ideology opposes capitalism as well as Communism, on the grounds that both stress material values over human values. Individualistic liberalism, said party intellectuals Gilson and Gortais, had provoked a concentration of economic power. As a result of the inadequacies of such liberalism, a philosophy of collectivism had arisen. But the collectivism of the Communists is just as foreign to the temperament of the MRP intellectuals as is individualistic liberalism. To their minds there is something insulting in the word "mass." Both materialism and individualism, said Robert Schuman, are generators of egoistic divisions in society and of social injustice.[1]

Within France, the MRP was consistent in its opposition to the tactics of the Communist Party. And in replying to Communist attacks, MRP leaders sought to employ reason rather than emotion. In early 1950, Premier Bidault had let the Communists show their colors in their strikes against Marshall Plan arms shipments. The party was aware that persecution of the Communists usually worked to the latter's advantage. But the MRP was also aware that more effort was needed to publicize the democratic way, as well as to show up the inconsistencies of the Communist tactics. To illustrate such inconsistencies, attention was drawn by the party in 1950 to the similarity between the Communist attack on the "imperialist" war in Indochina and its attack on the "imperialist" war against Hitler between 1939 and 1941 while Russia and Germany were allied. Note was taken that earlier in the 1930's the Communists had supported collective security against Hitler. As a matter of fact, Bidault had been called a Franco-Russian by non-Communist groups in France for seeking such a common front. And now, after 1950, he and other MRP leaders were being called Franco-Americans by the Communists for working with the United States toward collective security.

The MRP was not satisfied with being against Communism; it sought instead to be for something constructive. The party was criticized by the RPF in 1948 for not joining the anti-Communist front. In reply, the MRP declared at its annual Congress that Communism springs from the bad conscience of society, and that what was necessary to combat misery was a positive program rather than communism. French politics had need of a third choice, and the peoples of Europe and the world needed a solution other than that of capitalism or Communism.

The MRP took an optimistic approach to international problems that arose from the conflict between the capitalist and Communist worlds. To an unusual degree, it also steered clear of attacks on personalities. Again and again, L'Aube repeated the party slogan: "Le MRP sert la paix; il ne s'en sert pas," meaning that the MRP sought a policy of peace for its own sake, not for the advantage it might give the party.

Through its positions of leadership in the government, the party sought to keep France constantly in contact with Russia as well as with the United States. It was the theory of the party, from the time of its origin, that France held a position at the crossroads of the world. Therefore, France's normal function was that of a conciliator rather than that of a satellite. But acting as a conciliator, she should at the same time make her voice heard, as she had done in the initiation of the Pleven Plan.

The identification of France as a conciliator reminds one of the interesting distinctions made by Simon, an MRP intellectual, among the Orient, the Occident, and Europe. The Easterner, he said, lives in the bright and confounding light of the past and the American in the present and future. It is only the Western European, he said, who possesses a true sense of history and culture. Simon linked the European spirit with "mature conciliation." This display of ethnocentrism merits some consideration, although it is too much of a generalization. For instance, unless one were to distinguish meticulously between compromise and conciliation (as the author has done, in other connections), it should be noted that the French resemble the Chinese in significant respects, and compromise has also been typical of the Chinese.[2]

Maintaining a Bridge

The MRP represented itself, perhaps justifiably, as the most determined supporter of the traditional French pacifist movement. In France under the Third Republic, it is true, the only program common to all French parties was to avoid war in Europe. But after 1950, the MRP stood out above the others for its persistent efforts to keep a bridge open to the East. Tactically, the party leaders in the Government sought to avoid abrupt methods and dramatic actions. At the time of the Trieste incident of October, 1953, Minister of Foreign Affairs Bidault declared privately that France would not associate herself with the highhanded treatment accorded Italy by the other Western powers.[3]

The policy practiced by *L'Aube* illustrated the tendency of the MRP to de-emphasize international incidents. When an American plane was shot down by the Russians over the Baltic in 1950, *L'Aube* purposely refrained from playing up the incident. "The conflagration can be, must be, shall be avoided," said the editor, Maurice Schumann. Wars, he said, do not develop from incidents but from the relation between them and a general resignation to the fatalism of conflict. Again, *L'Aube* hardly mentioned the singing of "Deutschland Über Alles" at a German meeting in April, 1950, although the American press made much of this demonstration of resurgent nationalism.

Besides exercising restraint, the MRP was patient. There should be no closed list of possible agreements, said Bidault in 1950, or accusations that another country was seeking a third world war. In November, 1954, when Soviet Russia proposed a Big Four meeting, Bidault continued to exhibit his patience. He said he did not believe in automatically turning down any bid for a conference. On the other hand, the MRP opposed aggression "whether it be red, black, or brown." "We shall never sell our souls to the devil," said Bidault in the dark days of 1950 at the outbreak of the Korean conflict. But while diplomacy did not eliminate the need for defense, Bidault believed that the need for defense did not and should not prevent diplomacy. He demonstrated his ties with the old school of diplomacy when he expressed confidence that all difficulties with Russia could be solved by regular diplomatic means, or at least through present governmental organization. At this time, and at others, Bidault indicated a preference for secret diplomacy. If there should be "open covenants," at least, in Bidault's view, more progress would be achieved if they were not "openly arrived at." In his preference for the use of regular diplomats, as in other respects, Bidault differed from Robert Schuman.[4]

While MRP leaders attempted to maintain a bridge to the East, they realized that only from a position of strength could a useful (*libre*) discussion with Russia be held. Teitgen quoted Marx to the effect that Russia was a large beast that negotiated only with a larger one. To negotiate with the Russians, said Bidault, it was necessary to *faire face* (stand up to them). On the other hand, the MRP could appreciate Russia's concern for the security of her borders. To reassure Russia, Maurice Schumann, as representative to the U.N., suggested in a public speech in late 1953 that the West guarantee Soviet borders against aggression.[5]

In March, 1952, Russia had proposed to the West a treaty of peace with Germany, which would be diplomatically neutralized and authorized to have a national army. This seems contradictory on the face of it, unless it was meant to be an "army" for internal policing only. What Russia doubtless most intended was that there be a prohibition of any military tie between Germany and Western Europe. Borne doubted the seriousness of Russia's proposal of neutrality. But he said that this might be the last call for an understanding on Germany. Peace, said Borne, is otherwise called Patience (but he did not seem to be patient in thinking of this as the "last call").

The motives for the Russian proposal and the MRP reaction to it were not all apparent on the surface. Russia was seeking an alternative to the nearly completed European Defense Community. And from the standpoint of the MRP, negotiation with Russia would prolong the political minority of Germany. It would also put off the time for bringing into effect this unwanted child of European integration, the EDC. Schuman's continual attempts to keep the way open for negotiations on German unity retarded German rearmament. Here is a clear example of the contradiction between MRP words and deeds. The party supported the EDC and yet party leaders, even Schuman, would have been happy to find an alternative to it.

There was another reason for the MRP's insistence that France should not close any doors in her relations with Russia. During World War II, Maurice Schumann had pointed out that Germany had recovered so quickly from her defeat in World War I because the equilibrium of Europe had been disturbed by the exclusion of Russia. If the West and Russia could establish solidarity, he said,

German domination of the Continent would be impossible. Perhaps it was Germany, not Russia, that the MRP feared most.[6]

The most persistent MRP campaign for keeping the door open between East and West was carried on in the pages of *L'Aube*. In July, 1950, its editor declared that "even in the new circumstances of today" (Korea), the advantages of the Schuman Plan should be offered to the whole world without distinction or exclusion. When the Korean conflict broke out, *L'Aube* favored allowing China to send a representative to the U.N. Security Council meeting. Mao, as a "codisciple" of Stalin, could thereby serve to keep the West in touch with the Russian dictator. Moreover, China might eventually stand up as an equal to Russia. How prophetic this was, but apparently the time had not yet come for concern as to whether or not this would be good for the West.

Although some of the Russian proposals for a Big Four conference were seen to be bluffs to influence German public opinion, the MRP maintained that no occasion should be lost for an East-West negotiation. Borne argued that Russia did not want total war, although she was still concerned with her old search for sea outlets and the inciting of revolution in other lands. The chief danger lay in a "hardening of arteries" between East and West. At the MRP Congress of 1952, the *rapporteur* on foreign policy declared that one of the essential aims of party foreign policy was to renew the East-West "dialogues." There was a need, he said, for a specific interchange of ideas and goods between civilizations, rather than the triumph of one idea and one civilization over another.

MRP representatives in the Government sought continuously to put this party doctrine into practice. In his proposal for an Atlantic High Council in April, 1950, Bidault indicated that this might make possible the reopening of contact with Eastern Europe. Only the unsuccessful results of a four-power conference, he said in 1952, would finally convince the French people of the need for the EDC. "I don't see anything diabolic in it," said Bidault about such a conference, at a time when some did think it diabolic. With so much at stake, "no additional demonstration [of failure] can be superfluous." He persuaded Dulles not to postpone a four-power conference until after the ratification of the EDC Treaty and set out for the Berlin Conference of February, 1954, "with great patience but little hope." In Bidault's opening speech there, he stressed the preliminary need for a general understanding on the limitation of armaments. But when Molotov proposed a world arms talk, Bidault threw up his hands; this was too general. To one who preferred the older style of diplomacy, there was little chance of accomplishing something at such a widely attended meeting as Molotov suggested.[7] Bidault preferred the quieter way of negotiation, during which France would stand as mediator between East and West, preserving always for itself, in the event that Russia proved intractable, the chance to publicize the negotiations in order to convince a stubborn French public opinion that a new balance must be sought through European integration.

Within the MRP in 1953, Bidault was more inclined than other party leaders toward bilateral negotiations with Russia, thereby demonstrating the effect of his earlier contacts with De Gaulle. Later in 1953, De Gaulle argued that France was in the best position of any Western state to negotiate with Russia. "France is qualified par excellence," he said, since she had a treaty with Russia and maintained embassies in the satellite countries. The treaty referred to was the Franco-Russian Pact of 1944, which had been negotiated by Bidault and De Gaulle while the former was foreign minister under the Provisional Government of De Gaulle. In 1945, the MRP had referred to this treaty as "one of the imperatives of the peace." When Russia protested in 1950 that the proposed European army plan was a violation of the Franco-Soviet Pact, Schuman replied that the plan was purely defensive and that France would strongly oppose any use of Germany as a base for aggression.[8]

The MRP and Neutralism

In 1945, the MRP had expressed hostility to the idea of any antagonistic blocs of nations. It was in this year also that Bidault had said, "We shall never give our consent to a policy of 'blocs' more or less hypocritically opposing one another." The following January, Maurice Schumann, in a speech to the Constituent Assembly, referred to the MRP as the symbol and guarantee of exterior equilibrium for France between equally valuable alliances. Yet, with the coming of the Cold War in 1947, the MRP, in continuous control of the Ministry of Foreign Affairs, was unable to maintain for France this neutral position of balance.

The path of the party was all the more complicated because of the avowed neutralists in its ranks. It is a common saying in France that "at heart every Frenchman is a neutralist." But during 1950–51 especially, there were a few outspoken advocates of neutralism who were like the exposed tip of an iceberg. They believed that co-existence of the Communist and non-Communist worlds was possible and that Western Europe should serve as an international mediating force. MRP ideology, with its stress on the need for a third force, seemed to have much in common with these principles. Many neutralists, in turn, favored the MRP-sponsored Schuman Plan. Among the journalistic outlets of the neutralists were *Le Monde, L'Observateur,* and *Esprit,* and their principal leaders were Beuve-Méry of *Le Monde,* Bourdet of *L'Observateur,* and Étienne Gilson, one of the intellectuals and founding fathers of the MRP.

Many neutralists were Catholics, and most were anti-Communist. In fact, the paradox of the time was that Catholics in France were inclined toward conscientious objection to war, while Communists were developing a theory of "just" wars. Although Communists were violently opposed to neutralism, their party leader, Duclos, welcomed neutralists to "fight to defend peace at the side of the Soviet." Neutralism was a house of many mansions. The theme of many speakers was: "I am not a neutralist, but . . ." Although the neutralist party was badly defeated in the June, 1951, elections, it may have been ignored rather than rejected. When the MRP organ *Terre Humaine* declared that many of the newly elected deputies were basically neutralist but did not dare expose their inner thoughts, it may have been speaking of many of the party members as well.

MRP policy was directly affected by the growth of neutralism. For the success of its policy of European integration, the party needed to create the conviction of a strong Europe. There was a definite handicap to this in the danger of a revival of neutralism, the "Scandinavian disease," and the MRP itself was too closely connected with it. Gilson had been an MRP member of the Council of the Republic. Beuve-Méry had originally been on the board of *Politique,* an early journalistic organ of the MRP. Both of these leaders of the neutralists did not even approve of NATO. But Gilson was too high in party circles to suffer the fate of Boulet, another neutralist, who had been excluded from the party for voting against the North Atlantic Pact.

Some of the MRP leaders did take a definite stand against neutralism. Robert Schuman declared in 1950 that France could not and would not be neutral. Maurice Schumann called neutralism the oldest and most pernicious form of despair. And Bidault saw more danger in the neutralists' propaganda than in that of the Communists. Yet he said that the most dangerous of all were those who acted like neutralists and claimed not to be. In the eyes of Bidault, the neutralists had a "Solomon complex," feeling above the battle and oversimplifying problems. For example, Gilson had reasoned that the real victor of the future would be the nation or nations that conserved their strength rather than those that fought. But the weakness of the neutralist position was that it posited an unrealized condition—the autonomous force of Europe. It was this force that the MRP sought to create through European integration.

There were contradictions implicit in the disavowal of neutralism by most MRP leaders. They had opposed Gilson's main thesis that fear of Russia was exaggerated, and yet they charged neutralists with a tacit resignation to the inevitability of war. In other words, in opposing two contradictory neutralist stands, MRP leaders themselves were contradictory. Again, Schuman sought to distinguish carefully between neutralism and the willingness to negotiate with the East. Borne, in his turn, sought to draw a line between the more objectionable neutralists and those who did not want a new crusade to develop, or who were "realistic" enough to see the conflict betwen the need for social justice and remilitarization. Here again, a direct parallel can be drawn between neutralist principles and MRP ideology, which stressed the search for social justice. Party leaders found it difficult to deny neutralism without at the same time denying some of their own principles.

Gilson's neutralism was largely based on a distrust of the improvisations of American foreign policy. It was for this reason that he opposed NATO, although he had not opposed the construction of Europe as such. The Atlantic Pact had been a turning point, he said. Now the Europeans feared the obligation to support America in a war. Gilson pointed out that some American journalists most devoted to the "holy war" against Communism were the same ones who had, in 1939, favored a policy of neutrality toward Berlin and Rome.

One useful service of this neutralist movement was that it

guarded France against "vassaldom" in its relations with the
United States. But on the other hand, neutralism brought grist to
the mill of American isolationism, and, in the opinion of Borne, it
tended to drive the United States toward a reactionary capitalism
and chauvinism.

The "American Party"

MRP foreign policy, especially the program of European integration, was handicapped not only by the neutralism of certain Catholics within the party and by a neutralist ideology. Paradoxically
enough, the party's foreign policy also suffered because of consistent
party support for American policies. In fact, the MRP was given the
pseudonym "American party" by its critics, and, as a result, it
suffered indirectly from the extensive opposition in France to anything resembling a crusade against Communism. Many Frenchmen feared that such a crusade was being contemplated by the
political leaders in the United States.

The course of events after the beginning of the Cold War in 1947
forced France to choose between East and West. Through its chief
spokesmen, Schuman and Bidault, the MRP thereafter favored
close cooperation with the United States and Great Britain. Schuman called this cooperation the cornerstone of French foreign
policy. Bidault said that Europe could not save herself without the
United States, but neither could the latter maintain herself without
Europe. Through frequent articles in *L'Aube*, the MRP sought to
familiarize the French with the purposes of the Marshall Plan. A
cardinal purpose of this American aid, said *L'Aube*, was to dis-
courage aggression so that the United States should not again have
to liberate Europe.

The party was consistently friendly yet critical in its approach
toward the United States. The friendliness laid the party open to
frequent charges that it was subservient to the Americans. Opponents frequently made derogatory references to it as the "American
party." When Beuve-Méry was temporarily replaced as editor of *Le
Monde* in 1951 by MRP deputy Dupraz and Catrice—the publisher
of *L'Aube*—charges were made by the editor of *Esprit* that a con-
spiracy against the vigorous independence of *Le Monde* had been
stimulated by the demands of the American Ambassador. Again,

in March, 1954, when Bidault was still in charge of the Ministry of
Foreign Affairs, Herriot of the Radical Socialists was opposing early
consideration of the EDC Treaty in the National Assembly. He
disclosed a copy of a "timetable" prepared in Ambassador Bruce's
office and given to French officials. Herriot publicly declared that
"we cannot be threatened" by the United States.[9]

As can well be imagined, it was the Communist leader Duclos
who was most virulent in his charges of American influence on the
MRP foreign ministers. In March, 1953, he had called the EDC
Treaty and the coordinate Bonn Pact "treasonable agreements that
surpassed the treason of Pétain." At that time, Duclos had leveled
no direct attack at the MRP. But a year later, he charged that the
eulogy for Bidault by Secretary of State Dulles, at the Berlin Conference, should be dishonorable to a French foreign minister worthy
of his title. Communist tactics were typified by Duclos' quotation
of an unnamed American banker to the effect that Hitler had been
right in his plan to unify Europe. Bidault was called by Duclos the
"messenger boy of American policy-makers." Other critics were
not as personal in their attacks. But much of the criticism followed
the pattern of that of a writer in *Esprit* who complained that once
the French Government had accepted the "American policy" of
military resistance to the Soviet, it could not effectively refuse to
accept German rearmament. MRP leaders had striven to emphasize that the EDC project of armed defense was from the beginning a French not an American policy.[10]

There is no denying that MRP members of the Government kept
in close contact with the United States. Letourneau and Bidault
had accompanied Mayer to Washington in March, 1953, and Bidault was again in Washington in July at a meeting of the three
foreign ministers of the North Atlantic powers. At the Berlin conference of February, 1954, Molotov proposed a European treaty
relegating the United States to the status of an observer. Bidault
quickly declared that the "French people have no desire whatso-
ever to sever their tried and trusted friendship with the United
States." The American delegates accorded Bidault a position of
leadership at Berlin. Instead of altering the French reluctance to
accept the EDC, however, this American favor might well have
been the kiss of death for Bidault.

The critics who charged the MRP with subservience to the

United States should have taken into account the party's frequent demonstrations of independence of American influence. There were definite areas of irritation with the United States; all was not sweetness and light. *L'Aube* had been annoyed by the initial silence of the United States when the Schuman Plan was broached and suggested that America wished to recall the attention of France to the Cold War. Later in 1950, *L'Aube* attacked the isolationist stand of Herbert Hoover. It was Bidault's opinion that the only way to convince the isolationists of their error was to make a Europe strong enough to help itself. "One loans only to the rich," he said. Then Europe would be able to speak to the United States as an equal. The leaders of the MRP pointed out that the critics of Schuman's policy of European integration sought national independence from American domination yet simultaneously opposed the construction of a Europe that would pave the way for that very independence.

While supporting European integration, then, the MRP sought at the same time as much independence from American influence as could possibly be achieved. In early 1951, when Premier Pleven visited the United States, MRP leaders were disappointed at his failure to affirm such an independence. Borne struck a typically French note when he castigated Truman for having referred to Louis XIV as one of the earlier dictators. The "uncultured politician who rules in Washington" could not appreciate the Sun King, whom Borne rather puzzlingly called a "true lover of liberty."[11]

Criticism had been growing in MRP circles of the tendency to put the destiny of Europe at the mercy of the temperamental and nervous changes in American public opinion. "Everywhere in Europe," said Borne late in 1952, "opinion yields to the impatience and bad humor of the United States." America seemed to be intent on encouraging Moslem nationalism and the renaissance of Germany. In early 1953, relations between France and the United States certainly were not improved by a "terrific blast" at France in *Life*, which was soon followed by Dulles' warning through NATO of a possible "agonizing reappraisal" of American policy toward Europe if the European Defense Community Treaty was not ratified. Bidault talked back vigorously to Dulles at this late 1953 NATO Council meeting. Later, Bidault told the French cabinet that the United States had "demanded" ratification of the EDC Treaty.[12]

References to McCarthyism were conspicuous by their absence in MRP literature. Since there had been a general opposition in France to the tactics of McCarthy, perhaps the only conclusion possible is that the MRP was soft-pedaling any antipathy its members may have had to this political aberration in the United States.

In 1953, the British correspondent Werth hailed the "passive resistance to Americanization" by the French. "Many will say that France's greatest service to humanity over the past years has been precisely in this passive resistance. . . . There is a certain method in its madness." A poll taken in that year revealed that while the French generally liked Americans, they distrusted American policy. Bidault had taken a serious view of French-American misunderstandings in 1952. He criticized the loud opinions of American mass media of communication and inflammatory articles such as the story in *Collier's* of an imagined war between the United States and Russia. He also attacked angry outbursts such as that of Senator Connally's over foreign aid. The result of these, said Bidault, was an "instinctive human reaction" among the French, who were also worried at the haste of the Americans.[13]

The MRP Opposes a Crusade

Notwithstanding the frequent criticisms of the United States voiced by MRP leaders, the party was still regarded in France as pro-American and lost a certain standing thereby among the nationalistic French. After June, 1950, Bidault was careful to give credit to the United States for the effort made in Korea. He also strongly supported Eisenhower when he arrived in early 1950. At the time of the short-lived Paris demonstrations against Eisenhower, Bidault said that the greatest misfortune would be a break between the United States and Europe.

There was, however, one particular fear as common to the members of the MRP as it was to most Frenchmen. Not enough emphasis has been placed by historians of this period upon the opposition of Europeans to Eisenhower's roll-back policy. The French wanted no part of a crusade to liberate the satellite states of Eastern Europe. The possibility of this provided fuel for the arguments against the EDC. The MRP opposed also the development of a crusade against the Chinese Communists in Asia. In early 1951, Bidault

commented that if the United States sometimes suspected the resolve and strength of Europe, so also Europe suspected the consistency and wisdom of the United States.

In supporting NATO, MRP leaders accepted it as a purely defensive alliance and stressed its economic aspect. And in supporting
United Nations intervention in Korea, they nevertheless expressed
fears that such intervention might develop into an armed crusade.
A resolution had been passed at the meeting of the influential MRP
federation of the Seine in October, 1950, which expressed clear
opposition to the idea either of a preventive war or of the inevitability of war. At this time, Teitgen declared that all policies of collective security must depend on a distinction between wars of aggression and defensive wars. Toward the end of 1950, MRP leaders opposed any bombing operations across the Yalu River by U.N. forces
in the Korean War. "I am not sure the capitalist nations have clean
hands," said the MRP intellectual Simon, as he opposed the idea
of a crusade.[14]

The complications involved in the idea of a preventive war were
demonstrated in a commentary made by Borne in 1952. The occasion for his article in *Terre Humaine* was a statement made by
Monsignor Ancel that preventive war, "a customary cloak for aggression," is abominable to God and to the Christian conscience.
Before finally supporting the stand taken by Ancel, Borne demonstrated the dilemma in which some of the MRP members found
themselves. He compared Ancel to the conservative Goethe in that
both preferred injustice to disorder. Had one the right, asked
Borne, to be resigned to injustice because of the horror of war?
Even St. Thomas Aquinas had condoned morally justifiable wars,
and Péguy had declared that the will for justice is never pacific.
However, Borne pointed out that the assailant today always presents himself as a "liberator." At this point, he referred to the possible roll-back policy of the United States. Monsignor Ancel's statement might be distorted by the Communists, but a stand, he said,
was not good or bad according to who praised or condemned it. It
does seem however, that Borne as well as other Frenchmen exaggerated the significance of the roll-back policy, inasmuch as "liberation" was a campaign slogan of Republicans in 1952, and it was
fairly obvious there was no intention to use force to liberate Eastern Europe.[15]

In 1954, MRP voices were still being raised against a crusade. Hatin-Desgrées, writing in the influential *Ouest France*, said the strictest controls should be placed nowadays on the concept of a "just" war. The most pernicious groups, he said, are those that would set in opposition civilizations or ideologies. Bidault said, in the spring of 1954, that the French goal in Indochina was defense, not a crusade. He believed that lines of demarcation were necessary for coexistence, which he thought unavoidable in the present world.[16] But the support of MRP leaders for coexistence brought them up hard against a principle that was at the core of party ideology. This principle was that world problems could not be treated singly. That is, as M.R.P. leaders were fond of saying, "peace is indivisible."[17]

This was MRP ideology. But what was its practice? To determine that, we must turn to a detailed examination of party policy toward the former North African protectorates of Tunisia and Morocco[18] and toward Indochina, for it was there that Bidault met his Waterloo as foreign minister.[19]

6

MRP Policy Toward the French Union
and North Africa

"Peace Is Indivisible"

If the MRP could have concentrated on the French position in Europe, its stand on European integration would have been clearer and more consistent, and it would have become less involved in the disheartening Indochina affair. But Letourneau, the party leader most directly involved in the Indochina war, pinpointed the complexity of the party's problem when he said in 1950 that France could not play its role in foreign policy unless it was a world role. This attitude persisted; at the Lille party Congress of 1954, a resolution was adopted to the effect that internal economic expansion, integration of Europe, and development of the French Union and the protectorates were inextricably bound together. In attacking Rightist critics who said "Europe first" when one spoke of Indochina, or "the French Union first" when one spoke of European integration, Assistant Secretary-General Fontanet said in 1953 that a "policy of choices" was an alibi for cowardice.[1]

This doctrine of the indivisibility of France's problems was in effect a direct attack upon the thesis of Mendès-France that "to govern is to choose." It was this bête noire of the MRP who was instrumental in the elimination of party representation in the French Ministry of Foreign Affairs in June, 1954, when the Indochina issue reached its boiling point. In Mendès-France's booklet *Gouverner C'est Choisir*, the idea was developed that choices must be made and that among alternatives France needed first to ensure her own monetary and economic recovery. As an economist, Mendès-France did approve of the Schuman Plan, but he was indifferent to the fate of the French Union. This idea that alternatives must be chosen came into direct conflict with the MRP doctrine that

80

peace is indivisible and that France's problems of internal economic expansion, integration of Europe, and development of the French Union and the protectorates must be solved together. Support was given to this MRP thesis by nonparty political scientist Goguel when he argued that excessive conservative resistance in France would prevent internal economic revival without solving economic problems on an international scale.[2]

Time and again, the MRP leaders had clashed with Mendès-France on this issue, and their opposition was crucial when he was defeated for the premiership in June, 1953. They were opposed to his neutralism and his support for a cease fire in Indochina and believed that, in contrast to the MRP, he had no basic philosophy. Yet the younger members of the party liked the refusal of Mendès-France to indulge in ruses and equivocation and approved of his preference for an emphasis on economic vigor rather than diplomatic negotiation. The bitter opposition of MRP leaders to Mendès-France was most clearly demonstrated at the time of the votes on the Paris Pacts sponsored by him as Premier in late 1954. Bidault was said to be playing a cat-and-mouse game to force Mendès-France out after he took an unequivocal stand for German rearmament. "The night is ours," said Bidault, coming out of a three-hour party conference prior to the first vote. "We have decided to deal with you later," De Menthon had said to Mendès-France earlier. The MRP's purpose was to chasten Mendès-France; by a miscalculation, their opposition vote led to defeat of the Paris Pacts the first time. There was some caustic comment that the party supposedly most experienced in foreign affairs had opposed the Paris Pacts on the basis that because the EDC had obtained only 264 votes, no substitute should get more. It was a question of knowing, said an MRP critic, whether the deputies, "by their hatred of one man," were to break the Atlantic solidarity. When Buron and Juglas of the MRP leadership joined the Mendès-France cabinet in early 1955, they were in danger of expulsion from the party.[3]

The MRP doctrine that peace is indivisible was clearly a part of ideology rather than of practical party politics. Yet party leaders such as Bidault made much of it. Borrowing the phrase from the Russian foreign minister of the 1930's, Litvinov, Bidault applied it first to collective-security measures during the Korean conflict. The Korean test had to be met head on or others would follow, for

Communism knew no frontiers. But when the troops approached the Manchurian frontier, Bidault argued that the military activity was only part of a political affair and that other nations should restrain the tendency to "adventure." Hence, policy too was indivisible; the party had developed an all-purpose doctrine, it would seem. The Korean conflict also brought out disagreements among MRP leaders. Schuman favored stopping at the 38th Parallel. Bidault, remembering the Hoare-Laval negotiations of the 1930's, was for stronger action. Collective security involved collective sanctions, he said, and weakness encouraged aggressors.

Since Catholicism is inclined toward a universal approach to problems, one might be led to attribute this policy of the MRP to its Catholic character. But there was little dogma in MRP policy toward East-West relations; it was conciliatory rather than dogmatic. The party contemplated some sort of coexistence at a time when the Catholic Church was taking a consistently strong stand against Communism. It was only in its support for European integration that the party inclined toward dogma.

The effort of the MRP to handle problems on a world scale reflected an inclination in its foreign policy toward strategy rather than tactics. Schuman said in 1949, "If we can succeed in solving the German problem, we shall thereby solve the Russian problem as well." Bidault later said that the lesson of Korea was that the enemy should not be allowed to determine the place of attack. When one says No, one should say it quickly and specifically.[4]

The MRP Against Itself

In saying "No crusade, resist only the aggression of the Communists, but resist it everywhere," the MRP leaders took a courageous stand but a difficult and at times hypocritical one. This world system of the party made it particularly vulnerable to critics, both from within and from without. Any individual or group that takes a long-range approach to problems is equally subject to attack, though not to the charge of opportunism. Certainly, the MRP approach seemed impractical; how could everything be done at once?

The stormy petrel of the MRP, senator Leo Hamon, had raised this question as early as 1950. Of the alternatives, he believed priority should be given to rebuilding the French internal economy, and he clung to this opinion when interviewed by the author in 1954. He believed Mendès-France's *Gouverner C'est Choisir* to be a common-sense approach to politics. A nonparty supporter of MRP foreign policy also was critical of the party's "subtle complaint" that peace is indivisible and, being a strategy must be left to specialists such as diplomats.[5] The party often took on the appearance of being all things to all men in its foreign policy.

Even the orthodox leaders of the MRP were not too consistent on this policy. In contrast to Mendès-France's insistence that the Indochina war was incompatible with French authority in Europe, Bidault warned in 1953 that by becoming bogged down in Europe, France might founder (*sombrer*) there. She would thereby risk impairing her world mission. France's policy, he said, was to make Europe without *unmaking* France. Choices had to be made, therefore, but Bidault and Schuman would not have made the same choice. In an extremity, Bidault would have chosen the French Union and Schuman, European integration.[6]

There were other choices that the MRP had made. Although it had opposed blocs, it had had to make a realistic choice between them after 1947. In supporting the EDC, it chose to sacrifice its economic objectives for military objectives. The EDC was a project of very limited scope for a party claiming that peace is indivisible. Moreover, the Gaullists saw NATO as a forerunner of a German-American alliance. If this were true, support for European integration would represent a choice between that and NATO.

The most crucial choices made by the MRP related to its policy in Indochina and North Africa. Although it was the professed champion of negotiation between East and West, when French national interests were directly involved in Indochina, the party outdid its political competitors in stressing resistance rather than negotiation. And in North Africa, despite doctrinal support for greater independence for the protectorates, the MRP chose to submit to the pressures of the French bureaucracy and other special-interest groups.

Resistance in Indochina

Although the MRP prided itself on being the "European party," its leader, Bidault, found his stumbling block as Minister of Foreign

Affairs in 1954 in the tenacity with which he sought to hold on to French positions in Indochina. The reason lay in the belief that peace was indivisible. Letourneau, the MRP member of the Government primarily responsible for Indochina policy, asked how the West could hope to defend Europe after abandoning Asia. The Indochina outpost of Dien Bien Phu was strategic in the psychological rather than in the military sense, he said. If Indochina fell to the Communists, the rest of Southeast Asia would follow, and eventually all of Asia. How, then, could Europe erect a defense against these vast reserves of raw materials?[7]

The clamor arose in the National Assembly: "You can't do everything; you must choose." This argument, Bidault had said as early as 1951, was by its very simplicity pernicious and demoralizing. There is nothing more dangerous, he said, than clear, false ideas. Which should be saved, liberty in Europe or liberty in Asia? With his penchant for history, Bidault referred to similar criticisms against France's conduct of the Seven Years' War (which France had lost!) and to the arguments of Georges Bonnet at the time of Nazi expansion. How long would the French Union last, asked Teitgen, after Indochina was relinquished? In such a case, he foresaw (quite accurately) a chain reaction running through the other French territories. To choose one responsibility among several, according to L'Aube, often leads to the abdication of all.[8]

To know when to negotiate and when to resist in Asia proved a complicated problem for the MRP. At the beginning of the Korean conflict, the editor of L'Aube believed that China should be allowed to attend discussions of the Security Council. France wished, he said, to restrain the impatient ones who would "snuff out the glowing embers" (a rather injudicious metaphor) or crush underfoot the "broken reed" of international understanding. Yet, the succeeding editor, Maurice Schumann, emphasized that it was necessary to have a position of strength from which to negotiate. For those in the party who emphasized negotiation, the line of reasoning was that China should not be assimilated to Russia. The MRP leaders themselves, however, lumped China with Russia to the extent that they considered the French defense of Indochina to be part of the world struggle against Communism. And although one party leader predicted that negotiations with China would be lengthy for "such is the pace of things in China," other MRP leaders encouraged long-winded negotiations with China when they sought to have the Indochina question included in any conference to negotiate a Korean settlement.

Yet, little attention was given by the MRP to the possibility of negotiating a settlement with the enemy in Indochina itself. It is true that Le Brun Kéris contemplated negotiation with Communist China; the 1952 MRP Congress favored an international conference on Indochina; and Paul Coste-Floret suggested supporting the admission of Communist China to the U.N. in return for admission of Bao Dai's Indochina. But the heretical proposal of Denis in 1951 to negotiate directly with the Vietminh was quickly squelched by the party leadership. And Letourneau, Minister for Overseas France and later High Commissioner to Indochina, who bore the brunt of the Indochina war, concentrated on making war (often quite ineffectively) to the exclusion of efforts to negotiate a settlement.

The MRP, however, was opposed to internationalizing the conflict itself. Another Korea was to be avoided. It appeared that the party, believing that U.N. assistance would mean U.S. assistance and self-conscious of its status as the American party, bent over backward to oppose this development.

While Schuman, the Minister of Foreign Affairs, referred to independence as the final objective for Indochina, Letourneau and Le Brun Kéris saw membership in the French Union as a guarantee of independence. And, in answer to Nehru's doubts about the sincerity of the French goal of independence, the MRP reply was that the Vietnamese feared the departure of the French and that, in any event, France was fighting for India. Was not the road from Moscow to Paris, according to Lenin's prediction, through Peking and Calcutta? The Indochina war, said Bidault and Letourneau, was as crucial as the Korean conflict. Yet, the MRP wanted no outside help that would be likely to menace France's special position in Indochina. This put the party at an impasse.

The MRP in a Dilemma

Under the guiding hand of Letourneau, France was quite ineffective in prosecuting the Indochina war. Although speaking again and again of the excellent morale of the troops, Letourneau had accepted by May, 1952, the need for a native Vietnamese army. But he continued to resist actual recourse to international military assistance, which was authorized by a treaty with the United States signed in his presence in 1950, and when Schuman supported Letourneau's stand he was reproached by French senators. The National Assembly was also quite disturbed at the conduct of military operations.

Let us be explicit and say that the MRP, a party of policy-makers, had no efficient administrator, at least in the field of military operations. In the spring of 1952, Letourneau was criticized for unwise interference with military operations when he ordered an "unlucky advance," against the judgment of the military commander, De Lattre—possibly to impress Washington. There were continual attacks on Letourneau in the National Assembly, which in November, 1952, had demanded an increase in native Vietnamese troops (still conspicuous by their absence), negotiation of a cease-fire, and a promise of "independence" to subdivisions of Indochina. Letourneau's refusal to treat directly with Ho Chih Minh was attacked by the National Assembly, as was his tendency to raise questions of "face."

Criticism mounted against the MRP "wall of silence" that was substituted for negotiation in Indochina. Mollet of the Socialists had led a demand in 1953 for an end to "bloodletting," and the Socialist stand on Indochina complicated MRP tactics in June, 1954. In addition to this Socialist opposition, there were continual attacks by the Communists. The author witnessed a sharp verbal attack by Mme. Peyrolles on the Communist deputies in the National Assembly in 1954 when they refused to rise with the others in tribute to the soldiers lost at Dien Bien Phu.

There was also a widening split in the MRP over negotiation in 1953. The party Congress and Schuman supported international negotiation. But Denis and the perhaps more respected Monteil sought direct negotiation with Ho Chi Minh, asking why Russia would want to help France out of the mess.[9] In reply, the party leaders argued that Ho was merely a pawn in the Communist game. Negotiation with him would break the morale of the troops; only firmness would bring a satisfactory result. But firmness had led to the disaster at Dien Bien Phu. France was slowly on the way out, and rationalization had become the order of the day. For example,

Le Brun Kéris argued that the strategic value of Tonkin in the north had been exaggerated; Cochin China in the south, he said, was more important.

Despite the implications of the doctrine that peace is indivisible, most MRP leaders interviewed by the author in early 1954 opposed international assistance in the Indochina war. Although Bidault had approved direct American military aid in January, 1954, the party as such opposed this, referring to the contrasting national goals in Asia. The United States wanted primarily to stop Communism, the French primarily to stop the war. Yet, events were more demanding than doctrine, and Bidault declared at the Berlin Conference that France would "take any means" acceptable to the Associated States (Laos, Cambodia, and Vietnam) to make peace in Indochina.

Bidault made the penetrating comment that Russia, being on the offensive in Asia and on the defensive in Europe, would favor an accord on Asian problems more than on Germany. But there should be no *marchandage planétaire*, he said. The attack on Government policy in Indochina was often a pretext for the opponents of European integration.[10] In no event, said Bidault in the troubled spring of 1954, should settlement of the Indochina problem be made a condition for approval of the EDC Treaty. Asked in the National Assembly whether he believed Moscow and Peking would make free presents in Asia, he replied, "We shall see." In this "wager" of Bidault, said the political commentator Servan-Schreiber, the French national destiny was involved. Should the wager be lost, a neutralist Government would come to power.[11]

Before the wager was lost and Bidault was replaced by his arch-rival, Mendès-France (acting as his own foreign minister), in June, 1954, the West met in conference with Russia and China at Geneva. But the unity that existed among the Western powers at Berlin in February was missing at Geneva. MRP Secretary-General Colin commented bitterly that such a conference—until it met—was thought in France to be the best chance for peace in Asia. Yet when it met, its sponsors were attacked for evading the Indochina problem. Bidault returned from Geneva to meet acrimonious charges from Mendès-France in the National Assembly and demands for a cease-fire in Asia. The handling of the Indochina affair and the Geneva Conference were the immediate causes for the

ousting of an MRP representative from the Ministry of Foreign
Affairs after ten years of tenure.

The MRP National Congress, coinciding with the Geneva Conference, seconded the French cabinet in giving carte blanche to
Bidault, and Le Brun Kéris, *rapporteur* on French Union policy,
also avoided embarrassing their party leader. However, in an interview with the author just before the Congress, he had identified
the basic error in French policy as submission to American pressure
in the premature declaration of July, 1953, preparing Vietnam for
independence. Since he was quite critical of American tactics, Le
Brun Kéris was also critical of Bidault, who had given in to the
United States. In his report at the party Congress, he placed the
picture in a larger focus. The "master word" of nationalism, he
said, had entered Asia along with the "baggage" of colonialism.
And the French could not close their eyes to the growing importance of Asia and the weakening of Europe.

Retribution had set in: The Declaration of the Rights of Man
was being turned against its authors, the French. No movement
works always to the advantage of its originators; there is a balance
wheel operating in politics, as in all affairs of life.

North Africa: Assimilation or Association?

Although the average Frenchman would not have agreed in the
ten years after World War II that the relations with the French
Union or with North Africa fell within the realm of foreign policy,
there is no denying that they were inextricably interwoven with
general French foreign policy. For instance, France was careful to
see to the inclusion of Algeria in the North Atlantic Treaty area.
Moreover, relations of France with all the French Union except the
French Republic (which included Algeria) and with the former
protectorates, Morocco and Tunisia, were foreign relations even
before 1954. In Indochina, treaties had provided the original ties
with Laos and Cambodia, although a decree of the French Government integrated them in 1948 into the French Union as Associated States. An agreement with Bao Dai provided the same status
for Vietnam in 1949. In North Africa, the protectorate over Morocco dated from 1912 and that over Tunisia from 1881. Prior to
1956, the status of the protectorates was frequently confused with

that of the Associated States. Such was the situation when the MRP became seriously involved in French Union and North African affairs.

In contrast to the MRP's international policy of European integration, the keynote of its policy in North Africa was nationalism. In contrast to its claim to be the "party of tomorrow," it sought to preserve the *status quo* there. And in contrast to its aspirations to single-mindedness, there were inconsistencies in its North African policy plus disagreements among party leaders, which finally led to Bidault's exit from the MRP.

The party's nationalistic approach toward North African problems also contradicted its doctrine of pluralism, which supported the division of power among many groups in society with a resultant decentralization of control. In line with the French tradition of centralization, the MRP continually sought to preserve the authority of metropolitan France (the *métropole*). As early as 1945, the party favored building the French Union from above, not from below. Attempts by colonials after 1945 to take over French formulas of nationality were met with suspicion or derision. When an Algerian deputy sought moderately to invoke the principle of nationalism before the National Assembly, an MRP deputy chimed in with others to scoff at such "unheard-of language."[12] But the Algerian nationalists had held a strong tactical position in the Constitutional Committee of the Constituent Assembly, and the MRP was embarrassed in the spring of 1946 when De Gaulle favored a plan of decentralized federalism for the French Union. Even at this early date, the goals of De Gaulle and the MRP were not identical, as the party later claimed they were under the Fifth Republic.

At the second party Congress in 1945, a distinction was made between assimilation of the former colonies and association for the French Union and North African protectorates. While this new "community" did not require uniformity and the territories' "personalities" should be respected, no part of the Union should be independent in legislation or foreign policy. French sovereignty was to be maintained intact.

Since the MRP chose to use sociological terms such as "personality" and "community," "assimilation" and "association," it is fair to examine the meaning of some of these terms. Assimilation is a fusion of two or more cultures and is a two-way process. This did not seem to be the meaning of the word to the MRP when reference was made to former French colonies, since, as abundantly expressed in party circles, the intent was to extend all the benefits of the French culture to the colonies, and there was little consideration of a possible contribution in reverse. Association implies the joining together of equals, whether they be societies or individuals. As indicated above, this was not the intent of the MRP either. Finally, since the party had used the term "community" in proposing institutions for European integration, it certainly assumed the presence of political equality among the members. But the French Union and North Africa were intended to be special preserves of France.

At party Congresses, the MRP was either noncommittal or vague in statements on the French Union. Paul Coste-Floret, Minister for Overseas France, confessed at one point that although the French Union was a magnificent idea, he "was not sure just what it was or how it ought to be built." However, his speech at the Lyons Congress of 1951, although having "more 'blah' to the minute than usual," did reflect some effort at constructive thinking on Indochina, if not on North Africa.[13] In the latter area, the MRP was always "late with an idea."

Perhaps seeking to protect itself from the charge of being the "American party," the MRP expressed resentment at the "interference" of the United States in North Africa. The latter had supported the discussion of Tunisia in the U.N. General Assembly in 1951, at the time France was in need of more economic aid from America. At the party Congress in 1952, a resolution was adopted supporting common preparation for a new future *"respectant les personnalités marocaines et françaises."* But this was to be a preparation by France and Morocco; let no others interfere. The MRP was typically French in opposing any intrusion of the United Nations in this area. In the autumn of 1953, Maurice Schumann, French representative to the U.N., invoked the "domestic jurisdiction" clause of the Charter and announced that France would not participate in the U.N. debate on Tunisia and Morocco.[14]

No real step forward was taken by the MRP in this area. When Minister of Foreign Affairs Robert Schuman (who at one point mistakenly thought Tunisia was part of the French Union) declared independence to be the long-term objective for the French Union, he had to eat his words in a matter of days.[15] Even the party specialists on North Africa, Le Brun Kéris (on Morocco) and Vignes (on Tunisia), were not agreed on what steps should be taken. For example, at the 1952 party Congress, Le Brun Kéris supported internal autonomy for Tunisia and creation of a Tunisian legislative council, which should not, however, be allowed to prevent the inclusion of the French in official positions in the Tunisian Government. This plan was similar to the idea of "cosovereignty" that was popular in some French political circles at the time. But Vignes opposed such cosovereignty since he thought it would limit the goal of internal autonomy too much. He also did not agree with Le Brun Kéris that adherence to the French Union should be required of Tunisia.

The problems arising in North Africa were an acid test of the sincerity and effectiveness of MRP political philosophy, which stressed human values and the development of a higher international level of living. The party did, it is true, emphasize the need for economic and cultural development, and in the autumn of 1953, Maurice Schumann declared that, despite the heavy French economic investment in Tunisia and Morocco, over 90 per cent of the cultivated land belonged to Tunisians and Moroccans. But sometimes such stress on the development of these areas appeared to be an effort to compensate for Schuman's disregard for them in his concern for the integration of Europe. His demand in May, 1952, for an American guarantee of support for French policy in Africa and in the "Empire" [!] was a belated attempt to rearrange priorities as French parliamentary and public opinion wanted them.

The MRP was very circuitous in fostering the political development of the French Union and the protectorates. When it sought "independence within the French Union," more emphasis was placed on the "within" than on the "independence." Bidault did not favor a commonwealth status, since commonwealths had the right to secede. Maurice Schumann bleakly declared that a complete rupture of Morocco and Tunisia with the *métropole* would be a death sentence for France and would strike a fatal blow at the "Atlantic Community." Goguel saw one of the MRP missions as opposition to the "internal and selfish pressures" leading toward dissolution of the French Union.[16]

French individualism in political theory is counteracted by a worship of centralization in administration. By 1954, the MRP, itself nationalistic in its North African policy, had demonstrated a crucial lack of comprehension of the dreams of nationalism among the local inhabitants.

European Integration and North Africa

One of the most difficult problems for the MRP leadership was to determine the exact relationship between the contemplated European communities and the French Union, which would perhaps eventually embrace the North African protectorates. The MRP leadership in the Government had supported the maintenance of French sovereignty and security in Africa while sponsoring limitations on such sovereignty in Europe. Algeria had been carefully included in the defense area of NATO, while the European Coal and Steel Community, on the other hand, was made to apply only to European territories.

There was, however, a difference of opinion about the extent of the contemplated European Political Community. Le Brun Kéris favored entry of the French Republic (the Union minus the Associated States of Indochina) in its entirety into the Community. Otherwise, he said, there would be constitutional complications and also the danger that overseas territories might listen more intently to suggestions of a "United States of Africa." The adherence of Morocco and Tunisia to the Community might be arranged, should these two areas enter the French Union.

Bidault, although approving this plan in principle, favored only a gradual process of admitting the overseas peoples of the French Republic into the EPC. This procedure had been accepted by other prospective members of the Community. But the Quai d'Orsay did not want the Republic in the EPC and, as Minister of Foreign Affairs from 1953 on, Bidault was very strongly influenced by this bureaucracy.

In so far as the broader French Union was concerned the question arose whether the European Defense Community or the EPC could provide proper defense for the Union. Blowing alternately hot and cold over European integration, Bidault supported inclusion of the Union in the EPC. NATO, he said, extended only to Algeria, and, because of their interrelations, the EDC could extend no further; the EPC, then, would fill the gap. But he did not clarify how the EPC would handle defense problems. A related question was that of priorities: Which should come first, Europeanization or the rationalization of the French Union? To build Africa, said Paul Coste-Floret, one must first build Europe. No, said his twin brother Alfred (also in the MRP leadership); there would be no place in a "Europe" for colonies or trusteeships. Hence, there should be "stabilization" of the Union before its entry into the EPC.[17]

In this area, at least, the MRP did not really know what it wanted. It had become caught in a spider web of organizations that was largely of its own making. One of the most bitter critics of the party was Léopold Senghor, an African deputy in the National Assembly, who had earlier been close to the MRP. He emphasized the contradictions between the supporters of Teitgen, who favored integration of Overseas France into the EPC, and the bureaucracy of the foreign office, with which Bidault was frequently aligned. The "seigneurs du Quai d'Orsay" (who "traced their lineage" to Descartes) had sabotaged Teitgen, he said. France must choose the French Republic over Europe if she didn't want Overseas France to secede. Neither the French Government nor parliament should relegate the French Africans to the "stable."

If forced to choose between Europe and the French Union, many MRP leaders, including De Menthon and Maurice Schumann, made it clear they would choose the Union. The world responsibilities of France came first; if the French Republic entered the EPC, France should strictly limit her engagement.[18] When the chips were down, the MRP, the party of internationalists, favored national interests over European integration. But to avoid demonstrating the contradition between words and deeds, party leaders preferred maintaining the *status quo,* eliminating the need for a choice.

Since the party professed concern for the economic development of Africa—and in the light of 1957 plans for Eur-African economic cooperation—one should examine the Strasbourg Plan, formulated in the Council of Europe in 1952. This was a project contemplating a European organization for the development of Africa, including an investment bank, a preferential system, and long-term contracts on the purchase of raw materials from Africa.

"Beware of European neocolonialism!" warned Le Brun Kéris,

party specialist on North Africa. Only colonial powers like France, he argued, can become truly anticolonial. Thinking primarily of noncolonial states like West Germany, which predominated in the Consultative Assembly of the Council of Europe, he reasoned that each power had to pass through a colonial stage. It was the same old problem of the struggle between the "haves" and the "have-nots." Le Brun Kéris noted that the MRP had always insisted that the French delegation to the Consultative Assembly include Africans, to safeguard against just such schemes as this one. But besides all this, he saw handicaps to private investment in the proposal of a European investment bank.

Pflimlin, also disturbed about the Plan, called to mind the "European" propaganda during the German occupation of France and identified Semlar, a West German supporter of the Plan, as a previous champion of German colonial expansion. And when Italy suggested possible emigration to Africa under the Plan, Pflimlin declared that France was concerned with "civilizing" Africans themselves, rather than emigrants from other lands. Vignes, party specialist on Tunisia, in turn criticized the Strasbourg Plan for its failure to provide for a double preferential system (preference in customs duties to a European political community and within that, a second preference to the French Republic). Amazingly enough, he thought such a system necessary for the protection of French "infant industries" in Africa. Here again, a party spokesman demonstrated a contradiction between ideology and politics, supporting extreme protectionism as against the party's philosophical support for economic internationalism.[19]

The reasoning of MRP leaders was often quite circuitous in seeking to preserve French freedom of action in North Africa. Both Vignes and Pflimlin supported integration of the French Republic into the EPC for three reasons. First, France would thereby avoid special authority for Overseas France, which was unacceptable to the MRP. Secondly, they thought this would avoid the risk of a separate Strasbourg Plan. Finally, the risk of U.N. control over dependent areas would be avoided.

Despite support for integration of French Africa, Pflimlin elsewhere said that Overseas France in Africa should not be considered as the "common property" of Europe, but should enter the EPC as the "private property" of France. In contrast, Paul Coste-Floret had resisted the inclusion of the protectorates in the EPC, saying that France had no right to bring as dowry to a new Europe these fiefs whose titles she did not possess. For the organized economic development of French Africa, the alternative to inclusion in the ECSC or the EPC was the development of something like the Strasbourg Plan. But the MRP had objected to this, and in 1954, Pflimlin further complained that the Strasbourg framework was too rigid for developing long-term overseas markets. A party that had gone all out for the Schuman Plan for Europe now was playing a "dog in the manger" game in Africa. Doubtless, the Strasbourg Plan had its defects, but one gets the impression that the MRP resorted to the manifold resources of human reasoning power to preserve the *status quo* for France in Africa in both the economic and political fields.

Submission to the Fifth Estate in North Africa

In the spring of 1954, the North African situation was overshadowed by the growing crisis in Southeast Asia. Young Frenchmen were dying there. Many more were to die in North Africa in the future, but, as always, the future yields to the present in the public mind. The future came fast, however, and in 1956, the North African situation became acute.

In North Africa, as in Indochina, the MRP made a choice. Despite the implications of decentralization to be found in their doctrine of pluralism, party leaders submitted to the pressures of the French bureaucracy and other special interest groups, a fifth estate with strength overshadowing that of the fourth estate, the press. The result was hesitancy and vagueness in party action and policy. Vignes, for example, in commenting on Tunisian policy, said certain topics were beyond discussion, such as the "general interests of France" and the guarantee of the private interests of all French settlers in Tunisia. Yet Vignes, referring to pressures exerted by local administrators in the protectorates, opposed a new "Middle Ages" with bastions created against the power of any central authority. What Vignes did not realize was that MRP pluralism might well lead toward this.[20]

For pluralism has a two-edged blade. The division of power implicit in pluralism does not necessarily work to the advantage of the

majority of inhabitants of a smaller geographic subdivision. The
resident generals in the protectorates dominated the Quai d'Orsay
(itself *une maison vénérable*), it is true, but they were in turn
compromised by the irresponsible actions of local *fonctionnaires*
(administrative employees). Even more important was the dispro-
portionate influence of the French *colons* (settlers). By December,
1951, they had forced Schuman into reversing his relatively progressive policy. By his silence he supported the doctrine of cosovereignty, and he rationalized an association with Tunisia based on the
tradition of France, which he went so far as to call "a Moslem
power." In contrast, the MRP usually insisted on assimilation of
the Moslems into French culture.[21]

Opposition to Schuman in the National Assembly increased in
1952, precipitated by a military attack on Tunisian nationalists.
Although rejecting a Gaullist motion attacking Schuman's compe-
tency, the Assembly opposed the extent of the Government's proposed reforms. In contrast, some MRP and Socialist deputies criticized the inadequacy of the reforms. And when the Tunisian cabinet was arrested in March, 1952, Schuman was strongly criticized
by his own party colleagues for "having left policy to subordinates."

Pressure-group activity was responsible for much of the MRP
equivocation on North African policy. Cosovereignty had been the
suggestion of the *colons* for a new regime in Tunisia; this would
favor the bureaucrats as well. The danger lay in the "replacement
of parliament by the Government, and of the Government by administrative agencies." As the British correspondent Werth said,
the "crazy policy of the *colons* was allowed by the Government to
triumph all along the line." Werth referred to the strength of other
pressure groups besides the bureaucrats who were linked with the
colons, for example, the Employers' Federation and the Bank of
France. Lecourt, parliamentary leader of the MRP in 1953, referred
to the cosovereignty of the corporative trusts and the administrative
agencies. (A member of the MRP itself, Dupraz, was under a cloud
of accusations of being an *homme des trusts*.) As indicated above,
the MRP did not realize that such a situation might be the logical
outcome of an uncontrolled policy of pluralism. Division of power
can develop into fragmentation of power.[22]

Although Bidault as foreign minister did not try to escape responsibility for the actions of *fonctionnaires* in Morocco, neither

did he try to curb their actions. The only positive step some other leaders of the MRP took was to sign the manifesto of the Comité France-Maghreb, which was fighting the banking pressure group. As for Schuman, only after he was replaced as Minister of Foreign Affairs in early 1953 did he criticize the ineffectiveness of central authority in France. Since the Liberation, he said, France had been ruled by a *système collégial*, leading to anonymous decisions and mediocrity. In calm periods, the foreign ministers got credit and were blamed in the event of reverses. Schuman assigned the principal responsibility to the Resident General and recommended without delay a revision of French administration in the protectorates, with a return to the idea of exact responsibility of lower administrative echelons. "Our worst enemy is routine which knows only how to trust the past." [23]

Certainly Schuman had identified the principal source of trouble. But he had been Minister of Foreign Affairs for years; why had he not made a greater effort to change the situation? He had not blamed other ministers in the Government for misfeasance or nonfeasance but rather subordinate officials, many of whom were under his control. The early Christian democrat Lamennais had said, "He who despairs of convincing others either commits blasphemy against the power of truth or else lacks confidence in the truth of the doctrines he supports." Schuman had also criticized France for not choosing between various policies for North Africa. But in submitting to the colons, the *féodaux* (local administrators) and the banks, France and the MRP had made their choice.[24]

In 1954, Raymond Aron condemned Schuman's record on Tunisian policy, saying it proved his inefficiency as a foreign minister. Poher, MRP senator, based Schuman's failure on his excessive kindness to subordinates. To illustrate this, Borne told of an occasion when Juin, Resident General in Morocco, had seized an issue of *L'Aube* because it had published an Assembly speech by Schuman on North African policy. Anyone else, said Borne, would have taken immediate action against Juin, but not Schuman; nothing was done. Certainly these observations made to the author in interviews agreed with the impression the author received in his interview with Schuman himself—that of a kindly old man.

Part of the success of the MRP in retaining the Ministry of Foreign Affairs for ten years lay in the French political tradition of executive control of foreign policy, with little control by parliament. But by 1953, the tradition was losing its force. The MRP had to accept compromises in North Africa in order to hold the parliamentary support for European integration by the Radical Socialists, who were closely allied with vested interests. *Faits accomplis,* which had in the nineteenth century worked to the advantage of the Ministry of Foreign Affairs, were now being effected at lower levels. And if the permanent officials of the Quai d'Orsay made continuity in foreign policy possible, it was not always the same foreign policy as that of the political appointee, the Minister.[25]

Too Little and Too Late

The unorthodox editor of *L'Aube,* Corval, had declared that the notion of a protectorate was passé. "When your son has grown," says an Arab proverb, "make him your brother." In supporting the Sultan and the Moroccan nationalist party, Istiqlal, Corval declared that "we take our responsibility for this stand."[26]

Who were the "we" who took this clear stand? Not Schuman, who had opposed any interference by the United Nations, which had intervened on the Moroccan issue. True, before the Assembly Committee on Foreign Affairs he had supported the Sultan as the "natural middleman" between France and the North African people. But Resident General Juin, who had demanded that the Sultan condemn Istiqlal, was allowed to disregard directives from the Ministry of Foreign Affairs.

Was it, then, Bidault who had taken a clear stand? When he took over from Schuman in early 1953, his proposals on Morocco were full of generalities. Although he spoke of Tunisia and Morocco in "precise and generous" terms in bidding for the premiership in June, his actions belied his words in the August crisis. The French Government had been supporting El Glaoui, Pasha of Marrakesh, against the Sultan. Violence broke out in December, 1952, and the climax was reached on August 17, 1953, when the French Government ordered Resident General Guillaume to protect the Sultan. But this was of no avail; after a stormy cabinet meeting, the Government stand was reversed, and the Sultan was removed from his position the following day. It seems no exaggeration for an American commentator to have termed this a "ghastly mistake."

A week later, Bidault outlined a "vast plan of reforms," and sought the maintenance of French treaty obligations through an effort at reconciliation. The course, he said, was justified by the return of calm. But it was the calm before the storm. True, the MRP leaders followed rather than ordered what had happened. But Bidault, not wishing to oppose the *complot*, covered it up. While the Council of Ministers was considering possible punishment of the administrators who forced the Government's reversal, he said, "One doesn't punish people who succeeded so well." "They keep good step," said Domenach, "the children of the choir."

Domenach declared that in this Moroccan incident the extent of official lies reached the level of 1940–41, and charged the French Government with complicity with the United States. Mauriac declared that the breadth of interstellar space separated Bidault the minister from Bidault the journalist of the 1930's and called on the electors and militants of the MRP to learn finally to speak as masters of the party. But this was quite unlikely in such a centralized party. Boudon of the National Committee had said that if North Africa should leave the *mouvance française*, Black Africa would follow. "We have decided to defend our institutions," he said. The argument was advanced that the French took naturally to centralized administration and were not used to the idea of a policy for protectorates. But for Tunisia they had had seventy years, for Morocco, fifty years, to learn![27]

The rest was anticlimactic. In 1954, MRP leaders favored an increase in French police in Morocco but a change in their methods and the creation of a political party of French residents to undermine the influence of pressure groups. There was no particular progress in policy at the party's National Congress of 1954, where the author noted unusual politeness to the African delegates but relegation of French Union and North African issues to the last afternoon of the meeting. The MRP did not want to embroil itself over North Africa any more than necessary.

When Bidault initiated new Tunisian reforms in March, 1954, they were attacked by both sides, and terrorists became active again. Not until April, 1955, long after the MRP lost a footing in the Ministry of Foreign Affairs, was any accord reached on Tunisia. About a year later, France was forced to recognize the independence of Morocco and Tunisia, and by 1958, Algeria was moving in the same direction. If Bidault had stood behind the Sultan of Morocco, the chain reaction might have been prevented. But the MRP ministers in the Government delayed too long. Like France itself, the party was "late with an idea" in North Africa.[28]

PART THREE

7

MRP Tactics

Disadvantages of Participation in the Government

The MRP had to face the test of immediate success in 1945. The result was that its leaders were soon forced to play the political game; moreover, a middle course was more or less required of the MRP by its position in French politics. Cabinet members and deputies in the Assembly gained great importance in the party from the fact that the MRP was a Government party, never in opposition, during the first ten years of its life. But, at the same time, such a position of responsibility was a definite obstacle to the outward expression of the party mystique or ideology.[1]

It is little wonder then that, at least from 1953 on, many labor allies on the Left wing of the MRP, such as the members of the CFTC, became disenchanted with the party. The opposition of Catholic trade unions to the European Defense Community was based on the belief that it would lead to a disequilibrium of the Atlantic Alliance. In *Reconstruction*, the journal of the Left wing of the CFTC, the complaint was voiced that, instead of facing a Russian military danger and a German economic danger, in ten years France might face exactly the reverse.[2]

French labor groups are always prone to be suspicious of politics. In the earlier years of its growth, the MRP did not feel the effect of this. The party Congress of 1950 had included numerous workers, and, in the elections of 1951, about one-seventh of the total vote of the MRP came from the seventeen most industrialized departments.[3] In 1954, Goguel maintained that there were still more workers supporting the MRP than supporting the Socialists. The situation for the party should also improve, he said, from the disintegration of the Gaullists. But a change had already set in by the time of the exclusion of Denis in January of 1954. Denis had been careful to keep close to the laboring class. The MRP, said Do-

menach, had "chosen its companions," and now it had only a weak
link to the workers through Borne. Domenach charged that Borne
was condemned to live like a parasite within the party.

Nevertheless, Goguel maintained that there was a greater danger
that the MRP would lose the support of intellectuals than that of
the workers. Under the guidance of the editor, Domenach, *Esprit*
was moving away from the party. A referendum taken in 1953 revealed that 90 per cent of Christian trade-union leaders favored
the MRP-supported plan for European integration, in principle.
More reticence on this issue was found among the intellectuals
than among the workers. In all French parties, intellectuals are
more important than in those of the United States. The influence
of intellectual groups through the press in France is far out of pro-
portion to their numbers. Therefore, it is important to pay proper
attention to opinions expressed in the influential journal *Esprit*. On
the other hand, *Esprit*'s prestige is balanced by its small circulation,
which was about 15,000 in 1954. Mallet of the MRP Secretariat
looked upon the directors of *Esprit* as a tight little group of nonpolit-
ical philosophers.

The alienation of the workers and the intellectuals on the political
Left was not surprising, since any party that remains in the government for ten years is bound to become more conservative. Through
its retention of the Ministry of Foreign Affairs for that period, the
MRP had the chance to maintain the continuity of its foreign policy. But at the same time, the party was handicapped by its continuing position of responsibility. Bidault was Premier in 1946, as
well as in 1949 and 1950, and Schuman in 1947 and 1948. After the
fall of the Bidault Government in June, 1950, the principal MRP
members (Schuman, Pflimlin, Letourneau, and Paul Coste-Floret)
were returned in the two succeeding Governments. The following
year, Bidault, as Vice-Premier, became one of nine MRP members
in Queuille's second cabinet. The party again held the key jobs
in the Faure cabinet in 1952. Bidault was successively Vice-Premier
and Minister of National Defense, Schuman retained the Ministry
of Foreign Affairs, and Pflimlin held the Ministry of State for matters relating to the Council of Europe, which was about at the peak
of its influence. As President Auriol once said, "No matter who is
Premier, I always see the same faces around me."

The party had begun in 1952 to feel some qualms about the sig-

nificance of this continuing responsibility. When Pinay replaced
Faure in February, the MRP refused to take the ministries for
economic, financial, and social affairs. Although the Socialists were
anticlerical, the MRP had certain affinities with them in its ideology, and the Socialists had refused to support the conservative
Rightist ministry of Pinay. But Robert Schuman stayed as Minister
of Foreign Affairs, and Maurice Schumann and Pflimlin held key
positions. The Mayer Government of early 1953 again included six
MRP members, and the Laniel Government of 1953 and 1954 had
five, including Bidault as Minister of Foreign Affairs and Teitgen
as Vice-Premier.

The only government since 1950 that was headed by a member
of the MRP was, however, that of Bidault in the first half of 1950.
What, then, did it accomplish in its several months in power? Considerable criticism arose outside the party at its lack of accomplish-
ments. There was a certain justification in Reynaud's words to
Bidault, "Find a program or get out!" Certainly there was exaggeration in the Government's own proclamation that the Assembly
"could be proud of its work" and of the "prodigious and almost un-
precedented reorganization" that had been accomplished. When
the Bidault Government fell in June, 1950, it was the first time
under the Fourth Republic that a government had been defeated
on a vote of confidence.[4]

The Hinge

There is at times a certain value in *inaction*; hence, if the MRP
was inactive in internal affairs while it was in power, it was not
necessarily unwise. By retaining a balance of power between two
extremist groups such as the Communists and the Gaullists, it prevented such extremists from coming to power. French foreign policy was thereby steered away from the Communist line and, on the
other hand, from a reactionary type of nationalism. In the early
days of the Fourth Republic, the MRP was the only effective
counterbalance to the Socialists and Communists, and, from 1945
to 1947, "tripartism" was the pattern. The MRP maintained the
balance in these years and steered clear of too close an association
with the Communists. Although both parties had a centralized
structure, the MRP did not want otherwise to resemble the Com-

munists and, after 1947, consistently opposed them except in the case of their mutual distrust of and distaste for an electoral system allowing for electoral alliances.[5]

After the rise of the Gaullists in 1947, the MRP became a point of balance between them and the two Leftist parties. At the party Congress of 1949, emphasis was placed on the theme that the greatest danger for France was to be found in the RPF of De Gaulle, not in Communism, or else in the latter only as reflected through the Gaullists. Communism would play a key role in the resistance to this "new fascism." Hence, the MRP sought to avoid a swing toward extremes by keeping in power a government coalition of the middle parties.

Unfortunately, internal politics had a paralyzing effect on foreign policy, just as it had under the Third Republic. Occupying a place at the middle of a list of twenty-three parties in the National Assembly in 1948, the MRP had to maintain a central position to preserve its hold on the foreign office. The party managed to persuade the Socialists to stay in the Government until 1952. "Agreeing only on their peril, they could agree on nothing else."[6] The MRP, a party with a "red head and a white tail," had to try (in the words of Bidault) to "govern in the center with Right-wing methods to attain Left-wing ends." Its Right-wing methods included preserving contact with De Gaulle, although opposing the spectacular and provocative steps of his RPF. Bidault made it clear in 1951, however, that, although he regretted that the General had "bolted the door," he himself would not be the one to ring the bell.[7]

"Moving straight ahead by devious paths," the MRP sought by making concessions to avoid what Bidault called the old evil of domestic anarchy. After all, he said, "government is conciliation." By 1951, Bidault had become the symbol of the most conciliatory group in the MRP. In the early autumn of that year, he was accused by a party critic of compromising too much in connection with the temporary removal of Beuve-Méry from *Le Monde*. Suffert said that Bidault, "whose nose is so keen, smelled the wind and felt it freshen: It was time for the stroke of purity." Hence, Beuve-Méry was returned to the control of *Le Monde*. But thereafter Bidault was labeled by Domenach as one of the *double pensants* (double-thinkers). In foreign policy, Bidault was said to be "Atlantic in words and in acts, but resisting the Americans in extremities."[8]

Duverger had said in 1950 that it was time the MRP decided whether to remain faithful to its origins or move to the Right. The Center, he said, is a position that does not exist in politics. But, in late 1951, the party still acted as a hinge, since no majority could exist without it. Although it remained "faithful to its origins" in 1952 by abstaining from various confidence votes on Pinay, the MRP did not directly provoke the fall of any government in the first ten years of its existence. On the other hand, perhaps the party did not carry conciliation to such a degree as to make direct bargains with special interests, whose agents were expert in manipulating votes. The party made no use of the "black fund" of the strong Conseil National du Patronat Français. When Bidault was defeated by one vote in the summer of 1953, the lack of close contacts of the MRP with such business groups doubtless took its toll.[9]

Electoral Tactics

Much of the reason for the quick rise of the MRP was to be found in the electoral system. The Catholic party gained from the granting of suffrage to women, who are as a rule under strong clerical influence in France. Also, the *scrutin de liste* (vote by list) device had been introduced in 1945. This usually had resulted in voting for parties or programs, rather than for individuals, and had increased the influence of the centralized leadership of the MRP. In addition, this leadership had steadily supported proportional representation *sans panachage* (no splitting of tickets), since under the Third Republic the use of the majority vote and the "run-off" had led to an anticlerical alliance on the second ballot.

When the new National Assembly was chosen in 1951 under a revised electoral law, the MRP lost over 2.5 million votes and sixty-two deputies, retaining 12.38 per cent of the total vote cast. The story of the struggle over this electoral reform is a good demonstration of how motives can become confused but, being only indirectly connected with foreign policy, cannot be handled in detail here. Suffice it to say that for reasons of principle as well as tactics, the MRP, in its support of proportional representation, prevented the formation of a united front against the Gaullists and Communists. Despite the "curious alliance" between the MRP and the Communists on the issue of electoral reform, and despite feelers by Bidault toward the Gaullists, the party again reflected its tendency to prefer conciliation to compromise. Rather than make specific bargains, party leaders are more inclined to use the gentler, but more difficult, tactic of changing the attitude of other contestants for power.[10]

The more posts a party has in the government, the more its principles are bound to yield to a practical approach. In May, 1950, Étienne Borne, the leading intellectual and theoretician of the MRP, who was the party's main contact with the political Left, had contested the accusation that the party had fallen from the dynamism of Sangnier to the *immobilisme* of Guizot. It was necessary, he said, first to defend the Republic against anticonstitutional parties of the Left and the Right. Yet the party teamed up on occasion with the Left or the Right in the electoral battle, which was a little unusual for a movement that professed unconcern with temporary electoral reverses. The MRP was growing more and more jealous in 1951 of Socialist freedom from government ties. Even Borne was becoming uncertain of the party. In an article entitled "Should There be a Rebirth of the MRP?" he said that French political history was full of movements that had sacrificed the future for the present. A second foundation of the Mouvement was needed, declared Borne.[11]

In 1952, the MRP was being segregated into Christian democrats on the Left flank and what Duverger called "Christian Radicals" on the Right, despite its surface unity. The party was charged with supporting the Pinay Government, but with the visible hope of seeing it fail, which would prove the incapacity of the Right. But if this was the case, the plan of the MRP boomeranged. The Pinay Government was the turning point of the Fourth Republic. In a 1952 editorial in *Terre Humaine* entitled "Death of the Fourth Republic," Borne called the Pinay Government a return to orthodoxy and, at the same time, a return to control by private interests. Through its hold on the foreign office under Pinay, the MRP became part and parcel of this swing and, in particular, fell into an impasse over both Indochina and Tunisia.

Effect of Domestic Tactics on MRP Foreign Policy

In considering how the MRP managed to retain control of the foreign office for such a long time, we have found that the party gained some advantages from the postwar situation in France and also compromised or conciliated in its domestic policy. But, in some cases, it refused to bend very much, as in the cases of electoral reform, taxation, and the school question. This cut into the effectiveness of MRP foreign policy, since French governments still fell over issues of internal policy, as a rule.

The leaders of the MRP were constantly preoccupied with the danger of a break in the continuity of the party's foreign policy. At the Paris Congress of 1953, for example, Schuman intervened to defeat an attempt by the militants to condemn, post mortem, the Pinay Government. Teitgen, President of the party, also warned against going into the opposition, since it would turn control over to the conservatives, incur the risk of dissolution, and lead to a break or reversal in foreign policy. Throughout 1953, there were two majorities in the National Assembly, one for internal policy and the other for foreign policy. This delayed any action on the European Defense Community. Also, the problem of "freedom of education" handicapped MRP foreign policy throughout 1953. That question alone, said Duverger, separated the MRP from the Socialists. It is striking that partisans of the EDC were looked upon as Leftist if of the Socialist party, but as Rightist if of the MRP.

If the key to MRP compromises at home was to be found in its foreign policy, it must not be forgotten that the party also had to compromise in foreign policy itself. Schuman's policy toward Germany was one of "skating on thin ice," trying to satisfy both those Frenchmen who favored reconciliation with Germany (including himself) and those who were unable to decide which was the "lesser evil," Germany or Russia. He agreed to the unfortunate complication of the Pleven Plan for a European Defense Community primarily to get cabinet agreement on his European Coal and Steel Community. And when the European Defense Community was in the process of being drafted, the leaders of the MRP had to compromise again and again with opponents without and also within the party. There were those in the RPF who insisted on the separate existence and independence of the French Army. There was the indirect opposition of certain economic organizations. De Gaulle himself contended that "all great Europeans had been strongly national," as he threw his influence against the EDC. Within the MRP also, there were strong supporters of nationalism. The senator Hamon was dead set against a European army, deriding the "taste for the supranational" that was then in fashion. Hamon warned that peace was no safer with the reduction of the great powers to two, and he favored an independent national policy that was founded upon a development of the economic status of France.[12]

It was not only the "heretics" like Hamon who put such a stress on nationalism. Bidault had claimed to be a "federalist," but he made statements such as that in October, 1950, to the effect that the European army "did not entail any abandonment of national independence." He did, however, point out that a European army would reduce national differences and "sacred egoisms," which are, he said, equivalent to suicide. But Hourdin of the MRP helped little to reduce national differences when in December, 1951, he quoted a statement in the German journal *Der Stahlhelm* that "German blood and language are stronger than the idealist vision of the world imposed upon us."[13]

Most of the compromises that the MRP made on the EDC were either verbal ones, as indicated above, or compromises in time —in other words, procrastination. During the National Assembly debate of February, 1952, Heuillard, a Radical Socialist who had been crippled in German captivity, made a "dying speech" against any military commitment with Germany. This drew great applause and was influential in pushing through the National Assembly the conditions referred to in Chapter 4, which delayed the time schedule of the MRP. In September of the same year, Schuman was ready to submit the EDC Treaty to the National Assembly but was restrained by Premier Pinay. The following month came the "Herriot bomb" attacking the EDC. The MRP was incensed that the national debate on the Treaty had begun just at the same time as discussion of EPC had. But the party did not so much want a debate as to know where Pinay stood. With Schuman's acquiescence, Teitgen called on Pinay to say so if he was in accord with the Schuman policy. Schuman was ready to resign if the Government did not decide on debate by October 22.

This "sudden bout of political fever" in the MRP subsided quickly. Schuman agreed to postpone submission of the Treaty to the National Assembly until a preamble was completed. It appears that at this stage the MRP parliamentary group was more concerned about reconciling party words with deeds than was the party's Minister of Foreign Affairs, who had taken such a part in drafting the Treaty. Hence, another delay ensued. This was the time when Schuman was in such trouble over Tunisian policy, and he could not afford to get into more trouble with the National Assembly. On the other hand, he was too deeply involved in European integration to consider lightly the question of resigning. The rank and file of the party also refused to be stampeded into a decision for immediate debate on the Treaty. They did not want to run the risk of overthrowing the Government.[14]

MRP parliamentary tactics were continually complicated by the issue of the EDC. When Bidault sought the premiership in June, 1953, he left open the possibility that he would use the weapon of a confidence vote on the EDC. But in seeking the Presidency at the end of the year, he withdrew his candidacy when it appeared that the Treaty was being made too much of an issue.

To complicate matters more, the European Political Community had now entered the realm of discussion. Despite his coolness toward the EPC, Bidault was ready as Minister of Foreign Affairs in September, 1953, to give it priority over the EDC. His purpose was to get the support of former Gaullists, who would be free to vote against the EDC later. Bidault thought that the EDC could be ratified by a different majority. However, this seemed rather a fruitless maneuver, since at this time De Gaulle was opposing any EPC that did not include England and all of Germany. In contrast to his stand in the autumn of 1953, Bidault was distinctly cool to the EPC at the Berlin Conference of February, 1954, although emphatic in his professed desire to get the EDC Treaty ratified without delay. But in May, 1954, the party itself approved the postponement by the Committee on Foreign Affairs of a final vote on the Treaty, since it did not wish to handicap Bidault or reduce his "trumps" at the Geneva Conference. In secretly giving up the *ad hoc* Assembly plan for an EPC, Bidault had left the EDC an "isolated bridgehead."

We have seen that Bidault identified government with conciliation. As we trace his attitude through these postwar years, we are
forced to the conclusion that Bidault emphasized conciliation too
much. He was too yielding in his action and too devious in his
thought. Despite the many class and other group divisions, there
is a great degree (perhaps too great) of mutual tolerance among
politicians in France. Perhaps the "Republic of Comrades" of the
Third Republic is out of date, but not all camaraderie is. Ironically,
Bidault was repaid for his belief in conciliation by being attacked
on all sides while he represented France at the Geneva Conference
in the spring of 1954. Lecourt asked at this time what minister
could succeed whose least initiative was immediately suspected
and cut to pieces in his own country. The great weakness of
France, he said, was in morale and in such partisanship of the
press as would make the strongest nation weak. But it still seems
that what France needed most was a leader who had convictions
plus the courage of those convictions, and Bidault did not qualify.[15]

Compromises were also made, and principles gave way to opportunistic tactics, in the foreign-trade program of the MRP. The
party had criticized the individualistic liberalism of the French
Revolution, as well as the negative concept of democracy and the
tradition of resistance to government typical of the Third Republic. Yet, the MRP gave in to the individualistic liberalism of
French economic interests. Nationalistic trade restrictions on imports were being championed by party leaders at the same time
that they were pushing the Schuman and Pflimlin plans for European economic integration. In March, 1950, Schuman himself had
told the National Committee that there was need for France to
maintain her protective "dikes" for the time being. Later, Valay
and Buron pushed the expansion of agricultural exports, but reference to the necessary equivalent increase of imports was conspicuous by its absence. The development of French agricultural production, said Valay, was a "national and European duty."

The MRP had in fact provided in its program of June, 1950,
for a limit on agricultural imports that was very restrictive. The
necessary effect of the Pflimlin Plan on French imports was not
mentioned by a research section of party headquarters. Although
the MRP was pushing the Pflimlin and Schuman plans under the
leadership of Schuman as Minister of Foreign Affairs, new addi-

tions were made to French tariff walls at the contemporaneous Torquay Conference. The Government was also burying "without music" the Franco-Italian customs union.

It was misleading for the party to give the agricultural interests the impression that in the long run French exports could be expanded at the same time that imports were being reduced by the raising of tariff walls. Yet, this economic nationalism persisted in MRP federation meetings. *L'Aube* also opposed any increase of imports from Germany or any cutting of exports to Germany. Only Buron and Pflimlin insisted that internal economic revival and the organization of international markets were two aspects of the same effort. But the Pflimlin Plan did not escape the barbs of the critics. There were even some within the party who saw such plans as a form of escapism. They asked how supporters of his "green pool" hoped to deal with such men as Gingembre of the Petites et Moyennes Entreprises in wider European markets, when they lacked the energy and courage to deal with his type at home.

The MRP professed to seek expansion of social and economic democracy. France, said Maurice Schumann in 1950, could not choose between rearmament and social reconstruction; what good would armor be on a skeleton? If there were not a guaranteed minimum level of living, France would be extending an automatic invitation to Stalin to enter Western Europe. The struggle against Communism and neutralism must be one of acts, not words, said Secretary-General Colin; social justice is worth ten divisions. But during the ten years after 1944, there were constant temporizing and contradictions by the Government in its internal economic policy. Throughout this period, the important economic ministries, as well as the foreign office, were very often in the hands of MRP leaders. Goguel blamed the MRP for the constantly rising prices, since Buron, Louvel, and Pflimlin had steadily held economic posts in the Government. De Gaulle spoke for many, when he asked in 1951 how there could be a strong foreign policy with a weak and incoherent internal policy.[16]

Party Loyalty

At the same time that the MRP sought to perform a balancing act among the other French parties, it also tried to increase its inner cohesion. The degree of apparent unity and loyalty to be found in the MRP was surprising, in comparison with other French parties. The general homogeneity in the action of MRP members during the 1940's was based very much upon their common experience in the Resistance. Although the rise of the Gaullists cut the MRP adherents from 200,000 in 1946 to 100,000 in 1950, the result was a separation of the chaff from the wheat. Members of the party were not authorized to join the nonparty Gaullist organization named the Rassemblement du Peuple Français, but Michelet and Terrenoire revolted, and many of the party's electorate switched their allegiance. For those who remained in the party, precautions were taken in the MRP Statutes to insure that the action of party adherents accorded with official party doctrine, and that opinions of MRP members of parliament should prevail over those of the militants. In any event, the militants remained generally faithful to the party, except during the Pinay Government of 1952.[17]

There was, however, a certain degree of dissension as early as 1950. Pierre Dumas, referring to the dictatorial methods of party leaders, expressed the fear that party ideals would sink in the parliamentary morass and would be forgotten by leaders dozing comfortably in their armchairs. The Left wing, led at the time by Teitgen, was growing impatient with the influence of moderates on party policy. There was an incipient split in the party when the Bidault Government fell in June, 1950, and another under the premiership of Pleven. It is interesting that certain elements in the MRP were more restive under governments of businessmen, such as Pleven and Pinay. A party that had few contacts with business felt uneasy under such leadership. Militants were also tiring of enforced cooperation with the other majority parties. At the Lyons Congress of 1951, there was "something of a gulf between ministers and militants," as well as between ministers in the Government and some rank-and-file deputies, such as André Denis of Dordogne.

The result of the June, 1951, elections was a qualitative gain although a quantitative loss for the party, in the sense that a majority of those elected came from the less amorphous Left wing. In any event, there was a greater homogeneity in the party's following, except for such *enfants terribles* as Denis and senator

Hamon. But by early 1952, a Leftist faction was grouping around
deputies Monteil and Bouret over the troublesome issues of the
EDC. When the EDC plan was approved in principle by the National Assembly in February, six members of MRP were included
in the opposition.

A ticklish problem was presented to the party leadership when
the conservative Pinay became Premier in March, 1952. Only by
a close vote of 17 to 12 did the party's National Committee decide
that MRP members should join Pinay's cabinet; and that was on
condition that members of the party would not take the ministries
of finance, national economy, or social security. By April, Pinay
lost the backing of twenty members on the Left wing of the MRP.
Since the cohesion of the party was at its low point under Pinay,
it is worth while to examine the results of a study that was made
of the discipline and loyalty of French parties in parliament during his Government of 1952. With eighty-eight deputies in the
National Assembly, six of whom voted as a separate unit because
they were members of the Government, the MRP clung together
remarkably well. In 32 per cent of the "divisions," 5 per cent of
the party voted against the rest; in 7 per cent, the figure went as
high as 10 per cent of the party. Although the majority of the
MRP were against the Government 16 per cent of the time, they
did not oppose it in any "critical" division. In the Council of the
Republic where there were only twenty-four MRP senators, the
record was not quite so good for party loyalty. They voted as a
bloc in only 64 per cent of the cases.[18]

Despite the criticism of party policy on Tunisia by Denis and
Fonlupt-Esperaber, at the time of the actual vote on the plan of
reform, there was only one MRP member against the plan. There
was more of a split within the party over the Indochina problem.
When it came time for the municipal elections of 1953, however,
the party showed remarkable electoral stability. It was later, in
June, that a crucial test came in the National Assembly. When
Mendès-France made his bid for investiture, fifty-two of the eighty-
nine MRP deputies voted for him, although in many respects his
program was diametrically opposed to official party foreign policy.
The intricacy of French politics was partly responsible for this
tremendous departure from party loyalty, but even more responsible was the intricacy of MRP foreign policy. Many MRP mem-

bers abstained from the vote, only two voting against Mendès-France, who had with him the younger members of all the parliamentary groups. When Bidault made his attempt for investiture at this time, the party was solid behind him, with one exception (Denis).[19]

Considerable criticism was directed at the party for officially opposing its bête noire, Mendès-France. But the party pulled itself together again after this crisis, with only five MRP deputies opposing the National Assembly resolution of November, 1953, supporting the EDC. This lasted until the exclusion of Denis in January, 1954. By the time of the National Committee meeting in March, the *malaise du mouvement* was again the dominating spirit. Teitgen, who although moving toward the Right had been the most consistent of all MRP leaders in his support for the EDC and the EPC, tried to discount the classic distinction between Right and Left in France and to emphasize instead the influence of the bureaucracy against proposed reforms. But the more unorthodox Bouxom replied that the popular masses recognized well enough the existence of Right and Left, and the MRP should be forewarned of the support it would lose if it moved further to the Right.

Within the MRP, there had been expectations that the tenth Congress at Lille in May, 1954, would be one of reorientation after a decade of existence. But, as it turned out, there was relatively little controversy. A critic in *Le Monde* charged that the Congress was only disposed to hear the language of optimism, and that Borne's address skipped over the seamy side of party affairs. From an on-the-spot observation by the author, it did appear that the Congress went off much more smoothly than anticipated. The EDC was still the center of attraction in the discussion on foreign policy, and Lecanuet, chosen at the last moment to replace Schneiter, gave a good presentation of the party's arguments in support of it. There is no doubt that the Congress was generally behind Lecanuet, although respectful attention was also given to the critic Monteil, if not to Hamon. Opposition to the party's established foreign-policy program seemed rather fruitless at this stage. However, it was somewhat disturbing to the author to hear the automatic and rather mechanical ovations at the mention of the names of Bidault and, especially, Schuman. One was inclined

to glance up at the walls to see whether there were any huge picture posters such as are displayed frequently at gatherings of the
Communist Party.[20]

At the time of the final defeat of the EDC in August, 1954, only
two of the eighty-eight MRP deputies opposed the Treaty. These
two (Monteil and Bouret), plus senator Hamon, were soon ex-
pelled from the party. When the Paris Pacts for an expanded
Western European Union came up for vote at the end of the year,
sixteen MRP deputies finally did break away to give positive support to this project of Mendès-France. In contrast to this relatively
high loyalty in the MRP, 53 out of 105 Socialist deputies disregarded party discipline and voted against the EDC in August.[21]

Intraparty Disagreements on Foreign Policy

1. General Outlook. The over-all outward unity of the MRP
was unusual for a French party. But within, of course, there were
many differences of opinion that militated against the effectiveness
of party foreign policy. Frequently, these differences of opinion
were well concealed, as was to be expected in such a centralized
party, especially in view of its continued responsibility in the Government. To illustrate, during the debate of October, 1953, on
Indochina, Juglas had announced the stand taken by the MRP for
the vote. He was asked whether Minister of Foreign Affairs Bidault had not initiated a modification of the 1949–50 conventions
with the Indochina states. Juglas replied that he could not answer,
since he was a member of a government that had to be *solidaire*.[22]

But the contrasts were there, and some of them were based on a
general difference of outlook. Except for Schuman, leaders of the
MRP were quite French in their psychological approach to the
German problem. The fact that Schuman's early life had been
spent under German sovereignty altered his outlook. It was at
times used against him by non-MRP critics. During the National
Assembly debate on the EDC in February, 1952, Pierre André (an
Independent) said to him, "You, above all, do not have the right to
impose upon France what the people of Lorraine would call a mortal
sin." Several members of the MRP attacked the insinuations implicit in this, but Schuman merely replied, "I scorn your words."
As a matter of fact, it was Schuman who had stood alone, in 1950,

against the other eleven representatives of the NATO powers in insisting on the right of the French parliament to consider the "new" question of German rearmament and in opposing such a move until a European community had been created.[23]

In January, 1953, Schuman told an MRP caucus that he did not care to stay to be prisoner of a policy no longer his. He himself suggested that Bidault take his place as Minister of Foreign Affairs, and, after his appointment, Bidault declared that there would be no change in French policy. But Bidault's pursuit of European unity was far less ardent and far more qualified than Schuman's. "Let us hope that with [Schuman's] departure, Franco-German reconciliation and an authentic European policy have not been buried," said a political commentator. Throughout 1952, Bidault had been trying to follow a middle course. "Our memories and reason rebel," he said, "against an independent German army. . . . We deal with an emotional question that must follow its own course of evolution." Bidault was too prone to take a *laissez-faire* attitude on such questions. Would the course of evolution be the same as that which had led Europe from World War I into World War II?[24]

In his general attitude toward the construction of Europe, Bidault believed, then, in making haste slowly. He told the MRP National Committee in early 1953 that if a choice must be made between slowness and haste, he would choose the former. He thought it "not particularly scandalous" that such a great problem could not be solved today or tomorrow, and he discounted French fears of eventual German supremacy. Yet, the previous year Bidault had upheld the EDC, on the ground that if Germany were not rearmed in some way she would have a tremendous economic advantage. (Hence, economic competition was a motive for rearming a competitor!) As a former teacher of history, Bidault usually gave greater attention to the past than to the future. When it is a question of Germany, he had said in 1945, it is wise to take the counsel of the French.[25]

When Bidault replaced Schuman as Minister of Foreign Affairs, the MRP National Committee praised them both as "champions and artisans" of the program for a united Europe. But by the time of the Paris Congress of 1953, veiled interventions began to indicate the nature of the controversy between the two. Since

March, the party had failed to give strong support to the Schuman policy, which had been oriented toward Franco-German reconciliation and the belief that France's future lay in the leadership of Europe. In contrast, Bidault clung to the concept of France as a world power and placed the Atlantic world and the French Union first, rather than Europe. With respect to European integration, Schuman was primarily a functionalist, but he saw the construction of the EDC and of Europe at different levels. As for the EPC, by 1954 it appeared that Bidault would not accept it and that Schuman might have, but by then had become something of an opportunist. The two differed in another way. Bidault was closer to the traditions of French diplomacy; Schuman was lacking in respect for them. At the same time, he had a certain fear of the preservers of these traditions in their headquarters at the Quai d'Orsay. One should be cautioned, however, against exaggerating the differences between the two men, since all French foreign ministers have only a small margin of freedom in the actual determination of policy.

One thing that other MRP leaders seemed to agree on was that there was a clear difference between the approaches of Schuman and Bidault to foreign policy. Perhaps partly because he had been born and raised on the eastern frontier of France and had not traveled much, Schuman was inclined to stress the Franco-German problem. Bidault, the initiator in 1949 of NATO, emphasized that organization more than Europe. The contrast between the two was said otherwise to be that between *coeur* and *raison*—Schuman having heart and Bidault, mind. Less impatient, Bidault was more French in temperament. Schuman, on the other hand, knew Germany better, as a result of his language ability and his personal contacts.

2. European Integration. Although, in 1948, Bidault had emphasized political and military considerations in his negotiations with the United States on the creation of the North Atlantic Treaty Organization, party policy had always emphasized the economic value of NATO.[26] A basic part of the pact was considered to be Article 2, which provided for economic cooperation. Minister of Foreign Affairs Schuman had explicitly excluded the rearmament of Germany from both the immediate and future con-

sequences of NATO. But the MRP was finding it hard to decide whether the main goal of French security could be better achieved through closer ties with the Continent or by elaborating the network of relations with the Atlantic powers. Only Schuman consistently favored Europe. The lack of continuity in the shaping of party policy by other MRP members of the Government reflected to a great degree the fluctuations in American diplomacy.

Although he was closer to the Atlantic powers than Schuman at most times, Bidault was very critical of the United States in late 1950 (when he was not a member of the Government). The rearmament question, he told the Council of the Republic, had been posed by the Americans in the worst manner at the worst moment. However well-meaning these third powers might be, Bidault believed that their intercessions between France and Germany complicated the problem, and that Europe would be more quickly organized through agencies such as the Schuman Plan if others did not "mix in."[27]

Even without others mixing in, the proposal for a military pact complicated party foreign policy very much. Hamon was considerably justified by party mystique in saying that the economic challenge of Communism was of first importance. From 1954 on, this became increasingly evident, but some members of the MRP had anticipated this development in 1950, soon after the proposal of the European army plan. Hamon himself followed Mendès-France's principle of measuring perils and believed that the greatest danger lay in dealing with everything in military terms, which he thought led to increases in tension. Of course, party leaders tried in various ways to rationalize the EDC. In 1950, for instance, Schuman distinguished between NATO, with its temporary objective, and the European army plan, which, he said, was a definite solution and constituted a step toward a Europe.

It was at this time that Bidault cut the ground from under Schuman's feet by saying in L'Aube that a military effort toward a Franco-German entente somehow eliminated the charms of such an entente. Later, when the army plan seemed doomed to defeat, Schuman indulged in rationalization and drew a sharp line between the EDC and Europe. Teitgen was more consistent; he did not waver from his argument of late 1952 that Germany could not be chained forever. If she were not Europeanized, he said, she would be "Germanized." In answer to the fears of German hegemony in an EDC, Teitgen called attention to the fact that the German Social Democrats were denouncing the plans as an example of French imperialism. Only under the EDC, said Teitgen, could Germany subordinate military to civil authority.[28]

Bidault and Schuman were also at odds over the interpretation of the Bonn Contract with West Germany, which had been signed along with the EDC Treaty and was tied to it. Opponents of the Treaty were able to profit by Bidault's forthright acknowledgment at the Berlin Conference of February, 1954, of the significance of Article 7, Paragraph 3 of the Contract. This provided that a unified Germany would be able to accept or reject the EDC. Bidault stressed the international legal argument that a state could not bind a successor state to political commitments; Schuman, on the other hand, maintained that rights and obligations would pass automatically to a unified Germany, although treaties might have to be modified to include East Germany (but Article 10 of the Bonn Contract referred to the possibility of modification of that agreement rather than of the EDC, in case of German reunification). In the spring of 1954, Schuman announced his formal disagreement with Bidault's interpretation of Article 7. When Bidault appeared before the Committee on Foreign Affairs of the National Assembly, he explained that he considered this matter to be primarily a political question. A policy could not be imposed on a government that did not exist, he said, although he professed to have no doubt that a unified Germany would accept the EDC. It appears that Bidault was more correct when he stood on the international legal aspect. But since the EDC Treaty was a political one and would not necessarily survive until a new government was formed, both the legal and political questions coincided in this case.[29]

Although the differences between Bidault's and Schuman's approach to European integration were the most important, the opinions of other MRP *dirigeants* are worth noting. Alfred Coste-Floret, who was more active in support of European integration than his brother Paul, took a very independent stand during the National Assembly debate on the EDC in February, 1952. In Coste-Floret's opinion Germany was commencing a "balancing act" leading toward more association and less integration. Besides favoring more controls on Germany, Coste-Floret sought more action toward a political authority. He was opposed to as extensive a rule of unanimity for the Committee of Ministers of the EPC as was supported by Schuman and, especially, Bidault. "For us," said Coste-Floret boldly in addressing Bidault, "the proposed executive council of a political authority was more important than the committee of national ministers."[30]

Both Alfred Coste-Floret and De Menthon believed, in contrast to Bidault, that the French Republic should enter the EPC intact. Coste-Floret also favored creating the EPC prior to a revision of the French Union. De Menthon wanted closer ties of these European Communities with the Council of Europe and was unique in his support for a restriction in the powers of the projected EPC over foreign affairs. At least he was the only MRP member to speak out on this, as he did just prior to the adoption of the EPC draft by the Consultative Assembly of the Council of Europe.[31]

Bidault, as well as other party members, seemed to agree with critics to the Left and Right of the party who believed that a Europe of Six would be a strait jacket now that economy was expanding to a world scale. The Rightist RPF believed there was a need for world security alliances; the Jeune République, on the Left wing of Christian democracy, saw China as the coming power and believed that all Europe including Russia would have to unify against her.

Borne expressed the frustration of the MRP planners of European integration when he said that, instead of being a unifying idea, it created another point of discord. The nationalists, he said, cry against attacks on sovereignty, the liberals cringe instinctively at the idea of international organization, and the anticlericals suspect an idea is not modern that has not been condemned by Rome. The pacifists fear an armed Europe. How then, he asked, are we to make a Europe?[32]

3. THE SAAR. There were two disagreements among MRP leaders that involved, above all else, questions of parliamentary tactics. The first disagreement revolved around the status of the Saar. In the debate of November, 1953, Coste-Floret disagreed with Bidault, opposing a settlement of the Saar problem as a condition

préalable (preliminary) to the ratification of the EDC Treaty. Schuman (no longer in the Government) agreed with Coste-Floret that the Saar settlement should not hold up debate on the Treaty, although it might be a condition for ratification. (The original purpose of the *préalable* on the Saar, first required in early 1953, was merely to prevent the EDC from becoming effective before a Saar agreement.) Neither should a solution of the Saar problem be made a condition of the acceptance of the EPC, said Coste-Floret, since the *status quo* in the Saar was acceptable to France.

In March, 1954, Schuman suggested changing this *préalable* to a *suspensif* by simply adding an article to the act of ratification of the EDC, subordinating the exchange of ratifications to an accord on the Saar. Nevertheless, the official party stand, and that of Bidault, did not change. The private opinion of an MRP *dirigeant* (not, however, a specialist on the Saar) was that it would be worth it to hand the Saar over to Germany, rather than stir up trouble by trying to hold it. In other words, the game was not worth the candle.

4. The Question of a Referendum. There were also hesitations and differences of opinion among the MRP leaders on whether the party should seek a referendum over the EDC or support dissolution of the National Assembly if it rejected the Treaty. Either move would have been in line with MRP doctrine. In the Constituent Assembly in 1945 and 1946, the MRP had sponsored the inclusion in the constitution of provisions for a referendum and also had favored giving to the President a qualified right to dissolve the National Assembly. After 1945, the party continued to support greater use of the referendum in controlling the constitutionality of laws.

Here we are primarily concerned with the question of a referendum or of dissolution of parliament as it related to MRP tactics on the EDC issue. The tacit agreement to keep the Treaty on ice had been disturbed by the MRP as early as the spring of 1953, when party leaders, including Bidault and Schuman, took the stand that, if there were indefinite postponement of the issue, the party would seek a national referendum. Teitgen supported such a move if the EDC were rejected and no alternative approved by the

National Assembly. He favored a plebiscite either through a general election (which would have to be preceded by a dissolution of parliament) or through a vote on modification of the constitution, which would imply either acceptance or rejection of the Treaty. Lecourt made it clear, however, that the MRP supported a referendum, but not because the EDC was thought unconstitutional; in fact, he said that there was no such thing as an unconstitutional treaty in France. Teitgen believed that the referendum should somehow cover the whole policy of the construction of Europe, but it would seem that Teitgen and others had not thought out too well just how to pose the question.[33]

Lecourt apparently spoke for the party at this time, when he expressed a preference for a referendum over dissolution, since too many internal questions would be involved with the latter. Although the party had not conditioned ratification of the EDC upon the construction of an EPC, Lecourt argued that the referendum would be clearer if it included the idea of the latter as well. But such were the complexities of MRP tactics that this might make it less clear, if anything. No further important move was made within the party until, in his bid for the premiership, in June, 1953, Bidault hedged in his statement by saying that if the Treaty "were presented" he "would be obliged" to ask for a vote of confidence. But he favored dissolution of the National Assembly only if there were no majority for an alternative to the Treaty.[34]

In early 1954, the MRP finally made it clear that if the EDC were rejected, the party would go into the opposition to the Government. For the MRP alone among French parties, it seemed that dissolution of the National Assembly was preferable to a change in foreign policy. But they did not want to talk of a crisis before a decision was made on the Treaty. In February, the party publicly announced its intention to provoke dissolution if the Treaty were rejected, although there was some difference of opinion in the leadership as to whether debate should be begun before or after Easter. The question was solved by the usual procrastination of the Government.

In contrast to the party stand in early 1953, by the following May, a responsible *dirigeant* indicated to the author that the MRP had come to favor dissolution over a referendum. After some local electoral successes in the spring, the National Congress at Lille went on record that it neither desired nor feared dissolution, and the party was ready to demand it if inadmissible conditions were proposed to the continuation of the construction of Europe. But despite the protestations of the party leaders, perhaps the MRP deputies were too chary of their seats to push themselves out by a vote for dissolution. Certainly there had been enough time for these leaders to have fulfilled their threats, with the EDC issue hanging fire week after week, month after month.[35]

8

Between Government and Parliament

Turning now from intraparty disagreements to general party tactics in parliament, we find that, in general, MRP leaders were not as skilled in that arena as, for example, prominent Radical Socialists were. Schuman believed that the primary political purpose of his plan for a coal and steel community was to break down barriers between France and Germany. Unfortunately, MRP leaders were not interested, and hence not effective, in overcoming political barriers in the French parliament.

Except for Bidault, party *dirigeants* often demonstrated a lack of political skill when they sought, as members of the Government, to put into effect official party policy. MRP members of parliament were not experienced enough in the highways and byways of French legislative custom. When a delicate question arose in the National Assembly, the session was frequently suspended "to permit groups to deliberate," which led in effect to secret debate. MRP members appeared to be less devious than those of other parties in making known their support for, or opposition to, a delicate measure. This is merely one example of parliamentary habits that were frequently a handicap to the party, however politically moral its members may have been.

The MRP leaders did not take enough advantage of their political opportunities. During the National Assembly debate on Indochina in March, 1954, MRP speakers were conspicuous by their absence. This was typical of the situation in many earlier debates on foreign policy. To be sure, parliamentary time limits on debate usually gave the advantage to opponents of Government policies, and the MRP was on the side of the Government until 1954. A political opportunity that Schuman missed was the chance to get early support from Great Britain for European integration. The long-run wisdom of his policy of surprise in springing the

Schuman Plan on Great Britain is subject to question. The MRP was unsuccessful in its attempt to make up for this bluntness by formally seeking Great Britain's concurrence in the Plan in June, 1950.

An illustration of Schuman's inept political tactics is to be found in an incident that occurred during the February, 1952, debate on the EDC. Knowing that Socialist support for the EDC depended largely on the assurance of a British guarantee of assistance, Schuman did not act to contradict a baseless rumor that was published and relayed to the Socialist Executive Committee by Premier Faure to the effect that American and British guarantees were immediately available. (Most likely these were the NATO guarantees later ratified by the U.S. Senate, bringing the EDC under the coverage of Articles 5 and 6 of the North Atlantic Treaty; and the United Kingdom guarantee, relating to Article 51 of the U.N. Charter.) Schuman, having recently returned from a meeting in London, was also evasive before parliament as to whether he was to meet Adenauer there later. This was only one instance among many of Schuman's continuing reluctance to be explicit in his relations with parliament.[1]

It was also in 1952 that Schuman ran into trouble in trying to develop North African policy. The previous year, he had not tried to deny a charge by De Gaulle that a secret accord had been made with the United States on Moroccan military bases. Schuman suffered in his relations with parliament over North African policy because he was too uninformed on Africa, because he failed to give sufficient attention to France's world role, and also, perhaps, because he was too honest to take the anomalous French Union at anything but face value. Opposition to Schuman slowly mounted in 1952. In the spring, the foreign-affairs committees of both the Assembly and the Council of the Republic had expressed dissatisfaction at Schuman's methods, and the Gaullists kept up their attack on his Tunisian policy.

MRP political tactics were also rather weak in the handling of the Pflimlin Plan and the Saar issue. There had been no diplomatic preparation for the conference of March, 1951, on the Pflimlin Plan, and, with the fall of the Pleven Government just prior to this, non-MRP Laurens took over the ministry of agriculture and relegated the idea of a high authority to the background of the

conference. Pflimlin, inexperienced in the conduct of international
conferences, was also neutralized against his will by being chosen
to preside. In short, no decisions were taken at this meeting.

As for the Saar, when the issue came to a head in the spring of
1954, the attempt of Vice-Premier Teitgen to seek a solution in a
meeting with Adenauer at Strasbourg backfired, since Adenauer
advised Dehler of the Free Democrats that Teitgen was not sufficiently familiar with the details of the problem, nor was he authorized to conclude an accord. The German press criticized France
for sending Adenauer an "incompetent negotiator." A written
question was also posed to the French Government by Gaullist
Noel, asking in what capacity Teitgen had talked with Adenauer.

Most MRP leaders were deficient in the requirements of a politician. Schuman's gifts were those of a negotiator and a committee-
man, rather than those of an orator and propagandist. Somewhat
of an idealist, he went against the grain of many of the practical
French. Since he lacked the ability to handle Parliament, he sometimes disregarded it, as we shall see. Bidault, on the other hand,
had the essential requirements for a smart parliamentary tactician:
a brilliantly logical mind, a genius for formulas to bridge contradictory views, and considerable drive. But the complex technique
of the EDC Treaty discouraged him sometimes, and his occasional
fainting spells sometimes came at critical moments, as in his
speech of November 20, 1953. His greatest weakness, according to
Goguel, was a propensity for sibylline formulas and an inclination
at times to have too high an opinion of himself.[2]

Of a rather fiery temperament and reluctant to compromise,
Teitgen was less skillful than Bidault, but had strength based on
the ardor of his convictions and his ability as an orator. Of the
few who spoke consistently for the MRP in the National Assembly, it was perhaps Teitgen who made out the strongest case
for the EDC. There were some critics, however, such as Domenach, who attacked Teitgen, Maurice Schumann, and even Bidault for their "violence" at the least contradiction and the first
two for their inclination to indulge in "incessant hyperboles."

Inconsistencies and Contradictions of MRP Leaders

Besides the disagreements among MRP leaders, some of these
leaders contradicted their own statements over a short course of

time. It is probably impossible to take part in politics without involving oneself before long in some sort of contradictions in public statements. Even the more politically astute Bidault fell by the wayside in this respect at times. But Schuman was particularly prone to lay himself open to the charge of contradictions in his public commitments. Even in France, where political consistency is no necessary virtue, inordinate contradictions in public statements lead to a weakening of the political influence of the speaker.

After World War II, France, and especially the French industrial interests, became intent on the maintenance of international controls over the Ruhr. At a press conference on November 14, 1949, Schuman said there would be no increase in Ruhr steel limits. The following May, he insisted to a senatorial commission that his recently proposed plan was compatible with the Ruhr Statute, although it seemed obvious to at least one political commentator that the two were contradictory. In June, 1950, Schuman had assured the MRP National Committee that, regardless of the Schuman Plan, all control measures and restrictions placed on Germany would be maintained, but, in a statement to the same body in November, Schuman shifted his position toward the Ruhr by declaring that there was no question of changing the Statute "so long as the Schuman Plan was not in effect." If the Statute and the Plan were not incompatible, what then was the need of changing the former? Finally, at the time of the National Assembly debate on the ECSC, in December, 1951, Schuman took the stand that no ratification of the treaty could be effective until a deconcentration of Ruhr industries had been completed.[3]

As might be expected, it was in connection with the EDC that the greatest wavering was found in the public statements of party leaders. Not all of them would have agreed with Schuman's statement to the National Committee in January, 1951, that the European army plan was the *"conception par excellence de notre politique"* (nor did he himself later). During the debate of February, 1952, the Communists charged that Bidault and Schuman had protested violently in 1948 against the Communist contention that the break in the denazification program had meant the beginning of German rearmament. In July of 1949, Schuman had said that Germany had no army nor should it have any. A Communist speaker in the Assembly recalled that Schuman had also said, in 1949, that the Government would not accept any French grant of military bases in France to the United States. MRP leaders, who were usually quick to refute unwarranted assertions by the Communists, were conspicuous by their silence this time. However, there were few present in the Assembly that day, and, while Bidault and Teitgen were there, there is no evidence to show that Schuman was there to explain the circumstances surrounding his alleged statement in 1949.

It was also during this debate of 1952 that Bidault and Schuman contradicted each other indirectly in their efforts to do homage to the French conception of sovereignty. As Minister of Foreign Affairs, Schuman declared that he, more than anyone, was respectful of national tradition, but part of that tradition was the conception of generous and strong ideas. When he went further and said that it was the present pattern not to fight for a piece of land, a frontier, or prestige, but for liberty, he got scant applause. The following day (when attendance had dropped appreciably), Bidault repeated that France was being faithful to her oldest traditions in supporting the EDC, but he put it differently than Schuman had when he said that there are three things for which men die: their "little plot of ground, their nation, *and* an idea."[4]

It is interesting to examine the fluctuations in the pronouncements of MRP leaders on the subject of German rearmament. At a press conference in November, 1949, Schuman had declared there would be none, and he said the same in effect the following spring. When the question of common defense came up in the Consultative Assembly in August, 1950, Bidault said, "I do not know whether one day we shall be reduced to building a Europe that we did not intend, but I do not think that the moment has yet come to make such a grave decision." Just before this, Schuman had told the Council of the Republic that before considering arming Germany, France herself must be properly armed.[5]

But the idea of German rearmament in some form was slowly being accepted, "as men accept surgery performed on their bodies." In September, after having broached the idea at Strasbourg of a common control over European defense, Bidault rationalized his stand in a series of editorials in *L'Aube*. Without a European army, he said, national differences would be exaggerated, and moreover the defense of Germany would be impossible. The battle against Communism, if it must be, should be as close to the iron curtain as possible. In a press conference on September 6, Schuman hedged considerably on this question of German rearmament. The permission for Germany at least to provide basic materials, if not armaments, would not retire the permanent raising of the ceiling on steel production, according to the foreign minister. Moreover, an increase of the West German police force was necessary, he said, although a German army must not be reconstituted under the guise of police. In November, after the Pleven Plan had been advanced, as noted above, Schuman pressed for the ratification of the Schuman Plan treaty before irreparable mistakes were committed "based on the presumed necessity" of German rearmament.[6]

By the following month, the line between rearmament of Germany within a "Europe" and *German* rearmament was becoming very thin, no matter what Schuman could say. "EDC or the Wehrmacht" was, of course, not a very positive argument for the former. An important criterion for the distinction was the maximum size of all-German units. Scherer of the National Committee held out strongly against German divisions, and Schuman took the same stand in the name of the Government at this time. France officially went into the Paris Conference of February, 1951 (during which Germany was accorded equality of status), on the definite assumption that only German combat groups were contemplated. But by the following November, Schuman and the other French negotiators were accepting German participation by national divisions, thereby subjecting themselves to another attack by many critics, including Domenach of *Esprit*. Obliged to admit, he charged, that they have grossly deceived parliament and public opinion, they resort to a new *mensonge* (rationalization, or even stronger—lie); the number of divisions would be lower than that for France. And then, he said, *les malins* (the evil ones) put off to an undetermined date the setting of the numbers.[7]

Schuman had said early in 1951 that "active German participation [in a European army] . . . would lead to the danger of a conflict of which France will assume neither the risks nor the responsibilities." But his participation in the Government led Schuman around to the idea of substantially active German participation. Bidault, for his part, did not come out in flat support of the EDC until his speech to the Council of the Republic in

October, 1953. "The Treaty," he said, "was concluded as a result of a given situation which it is not in our power to modify. . . . It is a problem of conscience for each one of us, and I have spoken according to mine."[8]

Now that West Germany has been in NATO for some time, it is interesting to note the lack of consistency of MRP leaders on the question of such an expansion of the Treaty. In November, 1949, Schuman had flatly opposed German entry into NATO, and had clung to this stand before the Committee on Foreign Affairs at the end of 1950. But at this time Scherer had hinted, as a possible alternative to the European army plan, that German units might enter the "Atlantic forces." During the National Assembly debate on the eve of the NATO meeting in Lisbon, Schuman argued that the entry of Germany into the EDC would not connect her in any way, in law or in fact, with NATO. But in the spring of 1953, Teitgen pointed out that the army of the former was subordinated to the command of the latter (hence, France would not be "left alone" on the Continent with Germany), and the following year Alfred Coste-Floret was emphasizing that administratively the EDC would fall within NATO. Schuman offered no rebuttal to these contradictions of his statement.[9]

The MRP was apparently committed to the indivisibility of the Bonn Contract and the EDC Treaty, both having been signed at the same time. When, prior to their signature, assurance was sought in the National Assembly debate that the two documents would stand or fall together, Schuman replied, "I gave it in the Committee on Foreign Affairs; I give it again willingly." There was not the same firmness on the question of the British and American guarantees to the European army against German secession. Upon instruction from the cabinet, Schuman had set this as one of four conditions to the signature of the Treaty. He had previously said that the guarantees should have legislative backing in England and the United States. But the final decision at the time of signing was to accept a joint Anglo-American statement. This did not satisfy parliament, and in December, 1953, Bidault reminded Dulles and Churchill (who had supported the American position in Parliament) that the lack of an "ironclad pledge to keep United States and British troops on the Continent indefinitely" was the principal block to French ratification of the EDC Treaty. Little solace might therefore be taken from Bidault's earlier observation that "Great Britain has at least the curious habit of keeping promises she never made."[10]

The question of additional protocols to the EDC brought about more contradictions within the MRP. Bidault contemplated certain "lateral modifications" when he sought to take the Treaty "out of the refrigerator" in December, 1952. Additional protocols were presented by Bidault in March at a six-power meeting in Rome. But the opinion of President Teitgen in January had been that the Treaty should be ratified at once and modified later, and, in his March press conference, he refrained from commenting on the protocols. Bidault himself was quite equivocal in his stand on these protocols. He secured cabinet approval of them in February, and agreed at a six-power meeting that month to consider them as interpretive. But at the beginning of March, Bidault declared that the French parliament would not be asked to ratify the Treaty until the protocols had been redrafted (this, in spite of his agreement to press for speedy ratification). At one point, Bidault said that "the French intention is not to alter the Treaty but to render it clearer and more significant"; at another point he said, "The French don't know very well what they want" (he might have added "and I am French").[11]

On several occasions, Bidault sought to de-emphasize the supranational features of the EDC. By early 1954, the bug of sovereignty had also bitten Schuman enough to lead him to oppose any further supranational authorities in the economic field and to seek to dissociate the EDC from the "European idea." The Treaty "has lead in its wings," he said at one point. Schuman appeared to be seeking a back door out of the dilemma created by the EDC. In an attempt to explain French delays in the ratification of the Treaty, he said in 1953, "When a treaty is to last fifty years, all possible effects must be foreseen." Le Brun Kéris, in his turn, had argued as early as January, 1953, that a European authority could be constituted on the base either of a federation or of a confederation without supranational characteristics. As for the Dutch project of a "common market," Pflimlin raised doubts at this time about the wisdom of French support for it, and in February, 1954, Schuman said he believed it was going too far too fast to plan on commencing a common market before the sixth year of a European political community. This did not seem to be the same man who had presented the sudden proposal of May, 1950, for a coal and steel community.

Bidault, for his part, resembled a pendulum in his temperamental attitude toward Germany. In 1946, while Minister of Foreign Affairs, he had said, "Many things change with time; Germany is something that never changes." But in his speech to the National Assembly in November, 1953, referring to Germany, he said that "humanism and scripture alike teach that nations are perfectible." In the interim, he had argued that France should not wait until Germany was "again dominated by a power complex regained in isolation." In 1947, Bidault found Germany to be the major problem in the world; if there was an understanding on Germany, there would be an understanding on everything. If not, he said, "may God have pity on man."[12]

There was some lack of agreement among the MRP leaders on the question of the link between the German problem and world problems. Prior to 1951, statements by Schuman and others had been to the effect that German problems could not be isolated from others. But Maurice Schumann maintained that since the outbreak of the conflict in Korea, this was no longer true, although an agreement on Germany might lead the nations out of an impasse. By February, 1954, there was a full swing of the pendulum, and Bidault was distinguishing between Asian problems and European problems, at least, in the Berlin Conference. The MRP was seeking to dissociate the dilemma in Indochina from the dilemma in Europe.

Running to Extremes

A sense of balance is an advantage in most situations, and it is especially advantageous for a political party to maintain its balance. Instead, MRP leaders either were more enthusiastic than the political situation of the moment warranted or else were unenthusiastic for some party policies, especially the Pflimlin Plan. Party optimism was at its peak over the Schuman Plan. Maurice Schumann hailed it as the greatest victory ever achieved over the trusts. In proposing a treaty of fifty years' duration, Robert Schuman reflected extreme optimism. The surest economies, caustically commented a critic in *Droit Social*, limit their plans to five years.

Schuman's optimism in May, 1950, provided a striking contrast to the pessimism of Bidault, who had spoken in 1948 with "agonized bitterness" of the need for uniting "what remains of Europe," and who, as recently as April, 1950, had sought the alternative of further economic integration of the members of NATO, including of course France. We have already noted the lack of enthusiasm within the MRP for the EPC and especially the distaste for the European army plan. During the debate on the EDC in February, 1952, Schuman gave the "impression of following his project's hearse." Later in the year, when the much-respected Herriot of the Radical Socialists formulated detailed criticisms of the EDC Treaty, he charged that it was the MRP supporters of the treaty, not its critics, who had not read the document carefully.

By the time of the Berlin Conference of February, 1954, Bidault had come around to the opposite extreme, expressing overweening confidence in the success of the European army plan, which, he said, "virtually ensures against a resurgence of German militarism." Yet, during the spring of 1954, Bidault was criticized by the Socialist leader Mollet for failing to take more initiative to get actual participation of Great Britain in the army plan. The Government (including Bidault), he said, was more preoccupied with the reactions of opponents of the Treaty than with those of supporters of Europeanization.[13]

MRP President Teitgen was overoptimistic about the chances of the European Political Community. He predicted in December, 1952, that there would be elections for the proposed popular assembly within a year, and in September, 1953, he rushed to the Rome Conference to urge the French delegates to go to the limit of their instructions in preparing a political community. But Bidault's caution over this EPC balanced the optimism of Teitgen. Moreover, when the foreign ministers of the six "EDC powers" approved the principle of the Dutch "single-market" plan in February, 1953, Bidault opposed any appearance of haste.[14]

MRP enthusiasm was especially lacking for the Pflimlin Plan for a "green pool" for agriculture. Even before the Plan had a chance to gain momentum, L'Aube was discussing obstacles and reviewing reasons against it rather than for it. No attempt was made to suggest solutions for difficulties inherent in the project nor to stress its intrinsic advantages. Action by a high authority would be handicapped, said *L'Aube*, by two characteristics of the agricultural industry: a multitude of producers and the immediate effect a change of price had on consumers. It was forgotten that Pflimlin himself had not considered a high authority an essential of his plan, although the common impression was otherwise.

The conference on the Pflimlin Plan of March, 1951, was called on the initiative of the Council of Europe rather than on that of any MRP *dirigeants*. During the following year, the realization grew, within the party and without, of how the Plan would threaten the extensive French farm-subsidy system. Many troublesome questions were raised in the MRP organ *Terre Humaine*, one of whose writers summarized his pessimistic turn of thought by saying, "The idea of a united Europe is not yet completely dead." Only Pflimlin and Buron kept up the struggle within the party. The latter noted in May, 1954, that a minimum of organization was necessary to liberate the exchanges of Europe, and world markets were necessary to prevent the spread of Communism. Even Buron himself had emphasized, in 1951, the French (nationalistic) policy of encouraging exports, without reference to necessary complementary effects on imports.

On the touchy Saar problem, the MRP was, in contrast, over-optimistic. Perhaps with his tongue in his cheek, Schuman declared in the autumn of 1950 that the political problem of the Saar could be considered resolved. Adenauer demonstrated in periodic statements that this was merely whistling in the dark. Yet in July, 1952, Schuman again referred to the proposal for Europeanization of the Saar in a confident tone. In the spring of 1954, most MRP leaders interviewed by the author continued to be too optimistic, in seeing a definitive Saar settlement within a matter of weeks.

In September, 1953, Schuman had shown himself to be a master of understatement when he said that "any great enterprise has its moments of let-down." He found the three great obstacles to European unity to be nationalism, protectionism, and pacifism or neutralism. The belated nationalists closed their eyes to the evidence, he said, that nationalism was going out of fashion. He recalled that during his speeches, only once had nationalist demonstrators resorted to violence, and then they were recruited from a distance of 100 miles. Protectionism, he said, reflects the fear of the foreigner; "what was once a necessity in war has become a habit in peace." With respect to the fear of Russia by the neutralists, Schuman said that "to fit one's own attitude to that of an adversary is always detestable," and leaves the initiative to the adversary.[15]

"We cannot recognize the right of anyone to prevent us from being united," said Schuman.[16] Unfortunately, the right to European unity was omitted from the Declaration of the Rights of Man. Even MRP leaders themselves were not immune to the diseases of nationalism and protectionism, and part of their political philosophy was akin to neutralism. Hence, there was little reason for such rank optimism, especially since the MRP was building its policy toward Germany on the support of Adenauer almost alone within Germany. If he should die or lose control, chances would be much slimmer for the program of European integration. In the interim, MRP leaders lacked the energy to overcome the comparative indifference of French public opinion to foreign affairs. Schuman belatedly launched a campaign to publicize the EDC in January, 1954, but little more was heard of this campaign.

MRP Disregard for Parliamentary Opinion

1. PARLIAMENTARY PRACTICES. There is no denying that the most persistent and skilled tacticians would easily be frustrated by the temperament and practices of the French parliament. The National Assembly under the Fourth Republic was reluctant to take responsibility of any sort in the field of foreign policy. The deputies shifted responsibility to the Government ministers and then blamed the latter. For example, when closure of debate on the EDC was voted in February, 1952, by 327 to 287, over lively protests, a cry came from the extreme right: "Forty votes, forty ministers!" Although many interpellations were made and many questions were put to the cabinet ministers, few of the questions related to foreign policy.

There was some change, however, in the later years of the Fourth. It had been an axiom of the Third Republic that French governments never fell over issues of foreign policy. But in 1952, Faure made it clear that he would resign if the Government were defeated in the vote on the EDC. In 1953, foreign policy was the

decisive factor in the fall of the Mayer Government. When Bidault went out of office along with Laniel in June, 1954, the basic
issue was that of policy in Indochina.

Committees within parliament are growing in importance and
taking over control from individual deputies and senators. As is
true of Congressional practice in the United States, parliamentary
debate has to wait frequently upon the readiness of the *rapporteurs*
of committees, who are said by Howard (in his book on French
parliamentary practice) sometimes to regard their assignment "as
a means for the furtherance of their personal ambitions through
the production of monumental volumes." Schuman preferred the
relatively quieter control exerted by committees to disclosures to
the full Assembly, but committees could be quite troublesome
themselves. For example, Moch's Committee on Foreign Affairs
posed sixty-two technical questions on the EDC.[17] Even more
reliance was placed on committees after Bidault replaced Schuman, and some of the momentum of Schuman's earlier policy was
lost because committee decisions, like all group decisions, tend
toward compromise more than those of individuals. More bargains were the result.

In one way, the MRP foreign ministers, Bidault and Schuman,
had an advantage in the development of the economic phase of
European integration. This advantage lay in the relative ignorance
of, or disregard for, technical economic matters to be found among
most members of parliament. This is perhaps the result of the fact
that French legislation is much more general than Congressional
legislation in the United States; detailed implementation is left
to the administrative branch. But the resultant inadequacy of
members of parliament benefited MRP policy-makers only when
they could side-step the deep-seated political resentments of French
lawmakers, for many deputies in the National Assembly are psy-
chologically as well as technically unprepared to treat plans on
their merits. In the case of such a plan as the EDC, on the other
hand, MRP leaders ran up against the French disposition to fore-
see all possible dangers, which produced a sense of helplessness
and an escapist outlook. Many of the 628 deputies in the National Assembly were also frustrated and bitter, having risked their
lives in an effort to make France great once more.

Although parliamentary disregard for technical matters led to relatively little specific, direct criticism of economic projects such as the Schuman Plan within parliament itself, such criticism was not lacking. The critical function was taken over by the strong industrial pressure groups. It is very difficult to get detailed information on the activities of these groups, but it is at least significant that in France, more perhaps than in other countries, the fourth estate of the press is joined to the fifth estate of the pressure groups. *Le Monde* and *Témoignage Chrétien* are the exceptions among Paris newspapers in not being tied to any particular special-interest groups. Nationalized industries also exert pressures, but most important are the cartels, whose tight control of French industry survives.

2. PARLIAMENTARY ATTACKS ON THE MRP. During the National Assembly debates, the MRP leaders were the butt of many personal attacks by their opponents. Although these make very interesting reading in the *Journal des Débats*, they did not make the party's path any easier, and at times the answers of MRP leaders were rather testy. In the February, 1952, debate, the Gaullists made cutting jibes at them. Barrès quoted a diplomat who supported the EDC as having said, "The Germans long ago entered France in uniform; the political problem is to help them enter as civilians." Bidault rejoined, "Who is the imbecile who said that?" When Barrès referred to a proposal of a French general that special benefits be given to those entering into French-German mixed marriages, Bidault said, "Another imbecile!" Barrès explained that the author was Guillaume, Resident General of Morocco! The same day, Koenig (Gaullist) took a dig at Schuman, saying that in such a debate as the present one *l'amour-propre* (conceit) had no place. "Who spoke of that?" retorted Schuman.[18]

Of course, the Communists were specialists at this sort of diatribe. *L'Humanité* always called the EDC "German rearmament." In the above-mentioned debate, Billoux quoted Adenauer as having said on July 10, 1951, that young Frenchmen could die in order to return Danzig to Germany. "It is a lie!" said Bidault, "and you know it!" Communist leader Duclos referred to the alleged source, *Revue Intellectuelle*, which he said included contributions by MRP writers such as Hamon. Bidault insisted that it was a lie. "You lie!" said Duclos in turn, to which Bidault replied,

"Allez-vous en!" (Get out!) Duclos: "You work for Adenauer and not for France!"[19] Just before this, Malleret-Joinville of the Communists had asked whether the majority would "trample on the tombs" of 2 million Frenchmen, to which Bidault replied: "Taisez-vous!" (Shut up!) Finally, the Communist, on getting no acknowledgment from Bidault of familiarity with a certain bit of German news, resorted to an attack on the latter's health: "The particular state of fatigue of M. Bidault cannot excuse everything."[20]

In the debate of November, 1953, Duclos charged that Bidault was disregarding the Franco-Soviet Treaty, of which he had spoken so warmly in 1944, and also that the EDC could not qualify under the provisions of the preamble of the constitution, dealing with international arrangements for the defense of the peace. When Bidault quoted Article 7 of the Bonn Contract, which specifically subordinated the fixing of any frontiers to considerations of maintenance of the peace, Duclos countered with the charge that Adenauer had said in September that the first objective of Germany was a readjustment of the Oder-Neisse line. Communist aspersions were also cast at the Catholicity of the MRP. When the EDC was finally defeated in August, 1954, MRP deputies shouted at the cheering Communists, "Back to Moscow!"[21]

De Chambrun, leader of the few *Chrétiens progressistes* in the Assembly, gave frequent support to the Communist attacks. He asked, in November, 1953, why Adenauer had to be consulted before the French spoke to the Russians; as a result of the 1944 Pact, he contended, the priority should be reversed. To his argument that the Bonn Contract giving West Germany a certain status had not yet been ratified, Bidault replied that neither had the Franco-Soviet Treaty been ratified, although he admitted that it had been informally approved by the Consultative Assembly in De Gaulle's Provisional Government. A device used by all these extremist critics was the anonymous statement. Noel referred in the above debate to the additional protocols which, *"dit-on"* (one says), the highest *personnalités* responsible for French military security would judge of no technical value. Bidault interjected, *"C'est un 'on-dit.'"* Bichet of the MRP criticized the *protestations fabriquées* that Noel said had been coming from local patriotic and military organizations.[22]

The temper of the French National Assembly is like that of no other legislature in the world, and these illustrations may partly explain the reluctance of MRP ministers to descend into the arena and seek Assembly approval of their foreign policy. There is an aura of mistrust among French politicians. It is perhaps significant that to the French greeting *"Comment va?"* the typical answer is *"On se défend."*

3. Avoidance of Parliament by MRP Leaders. Although the level of much of the criticism in the National Assembly might provide a partial explanation for the MRP leaders' avoidance of that body, they were tactically unwise in failing to take the sensibilities of both branches of parliament into account. There was, for example, a striking failure to prepare parliamentary opinion, and also public opinion within France, for the Schuman Plan. Furthermore, in June, 1950, Schuman opposed a resolution in the National Assembly requiring preliminary agreement on the negotiations by parliament, explaining in the debate the following month that he was willing to give information but that he could not tie his hands in the middle of negotiations. He promised, however, that there would be no *faits accomplis* and that the Assembly would have a full chance to make its decision.

Bidault, in his turn, frequently showed that he preferred the channels and methods of traditional diplomacy in developing foreign policy. In September, 1950, he criticized the intense publicity of the negotiations over the project for a European army, referring to such publicity as "one of the superstitions of today." What was necessary were decisions, not talk, he said, if the West were to take the initiative away from Russia. There was nothing worse in a dangerous situation, said Bidault, than announcing a course that could not yet be taken; it smacked of internal politics. Yet the very reason for the demand for publicity and discussion that displeased Bidault may have been the too frequent attempts of Schuman to disregard parliament and keep the negotiations on the European army quiet.

In a country like France, where members of the legislature prided themselves on independence of thought, disregard for them was always dangerous in the Fourth Republic, regardless of the fact that until recently they had concentrated their attention on internal affairs. Perhaps parliament in France was so difficult to handle because its members sensed the decline in the importance of the legislature and reacted with frustration. During the campaign for a European parliament under the EDC, a writer in a French journal commented that it made one smile sadly, for "we no longer believe in parliamentarism except in opposing dictatorship." French governmental instability had led to an increase in the power of permanent officials not responsible to parliament and also to a disaffection for parliamentary government. There was a growing *"dépossession du Parlement par le Gouvernement, du Gouvernement par les bureaux."*[23]

In a declaration to the Assembly on August 30, 1951, Schuman referred to Briand's inability in 1929 to announce his stand on the coming negotiations at the Hague and said that he was faithful to Briand's rule. A debate, said Schuman, would involve statements that would tend to bind the negotiators and therefore could not be accepted; it was the Government that was responsible for negotiations. It was the function of parliament to accept or not the results of the negotiations, not to give instructions that would handicap the negotiators. By the vote of investiture of the Premier, the Assembly had, according to Schuman's argument, accepted the general policy of the Government. In contrast to Bidault, who was inclined to rely on the diplomats, Schuman seemed to rely on himself.

Even an MRP writer in *Terre Humaine* declared in 1951 that there seemed never to have been such a split between official policy and the reactions of the French. He found the answer in the traditions of secret diplomacy supported by Schuman, who refused to take any precise directives from the deputies. In that year, Schuman told the National Assembly that there would be no *fait accompli*, nor were there any moral commitments on the European army plan before a parliamentary debate. Yet, the following month, after announcing "very great progress" at the meeting of the six foreign ministers at Strasbourg, Schuman stated that "we all made concessions," and now it was "certain" that a supranational authority would be set up to run the army. Opening the debate in the National Assembly in February, Schuman reminded his listeners that he had said several times that it was "not the function of parliament to intervene in negotiations in process";

this was an executive function, and in interfering with it there was the danger of creating a precedent. But the gravity of the situation had led the Government, he said, to seek this debate.

In this debate, Schuman urged the deputies to "reflect without passion," but his audience was generally unenthusiastic, to say the least. The violent opposition to the EDC on both the Left and Right of the Assembly had not been expressed much until this time because of the relative secrecy of the negotiations. It was only a week before the debate that the foreign office had finally circulated a summary of the project.[24] And from the time the EDC Treaty was finally signed in May, 1952, to the following January, Schuman kept the treaty "in his briefcase," never adequately explaining the delay. Up until that time, when it was finally submitted to parliament the Government had not approved the deposition of the Treaty in parliament for ratification.

Again, in April, 1954, MRP Minister of Foreign Affairs Bidault was charged with disregarding parliament. Conventions with Great Britain had been signed that committed the latter to a definite amount of military support on the Continent for a determinate period of time. However, these were presented to the French cabinet by Bidault and Teitgen in such a manner as seemed to some critics to force the hands of the ministers and the National Assembly. Some ministers had seen the text only an hour previously, and adversaries also protested the holding back of the text until the National Assembly was on its extended Easter recess.[25]

4. COMMITTING PARLIAMENT. As early as January, 1950, the National Assembly itself had required that under no circumstances should West Germany be allowed the reconstitution of her military forces, and after the February, 1952, debate on the European army plan and upon the demand of the Socialists, the National Assembly set five specific conditions for the ratification of the EDC Treaty. Once the treaty had been signed, however, Schuman was persistent in his demand that the Government defend it. At the MRP Congress of 1953, after he had left the foreign office, he declared that a government does not have the right to fail to defend a treaty it has signed, referring apparently to the French Government, rather than to any particular government of any one premier. In the debate of November, 1953, speaking as a deputy,

Schuman declared that he remained faithful to the policy that "we" had commenced. But Bonnefous, formerly head of the Committee on Foreign Affairs, took the occasion in this debate to criticize the idea that France was committed to the EDC because it had given its signature to the Treaty. For example, deputies would be particularly concerned over the fact that the purchasing power that the Commissariat of the Community would have over armaments would deprive the Assembly of some control over the national budget. It is significant to note that the chairmen of the two commissions most concerned with the Treaty were against it.

Schuman's failure to be more solicitous of British sensibilities in drafting the Schuman Plan also had later repercussions in parliament, since powerful elements of the National Assembly, particularly the Socialists, were opposed to a Europe without England. During the embryonic discussions of a European political community in the fall of 1950, Schuman was more concerned about England's attitude and called on the British to form part of this united Europe. His effort was nipped in the bud, however, by a semiofficial statement from the French Government saying it had not yet considered the question. (Schuman was discovering that he could not drag France along in his wake.) In the autumn of 1952, Schuman favored drafting a charter for the EPC under the auspices of the Council of Europe, since such procedure conformed "with English views." In his address to the National Assembly in 1953, supporting the need for bringing Great Britain into the EDC, Bidault said that Great Britain would rather keep engagements than sign them.[26]

5. MRP WEAKNESS IN DEBATE. In the actual debates in the National Assembly, which were few and far between so far as foreign policy was concerned, MRP participation was somewhat wanting, to say the least. Perhaps Teitgen gave the best account of himself; to the objections raised against the Pleven Plan in the early debate of October, 1950, for example, he replied at length, and in an optimistic manner. There was something more pessimistic in the quality of Schuman's address to the National Assembly in February, 1952. Except for Teitgen, a very limited number of speeches were made by MRP members in parliament in support of the program of European construction. Despite the extenuating

explanations to be found in parliamentary rules, the net result was a weakening of the MRP case as the opposition increased in tempo. This effect was accentuated by the infrequency of debates; at the time of the signature of the EDC Treaty, a debate that had been asked for was not even on the calendar, and although the *projet de loi* was submitted to the Assembly in January, 1953, the next debate did not come until the following November. And then Bidault's fainting spell was an ill omen and especially unfortunate since his well-drafted defense of the EDC lost its effect.[27]

Ardent reformers such as Jean Monnet (who drafted the details of the Schuman Plan) and, to a lesser degree, Schuman usually preferred to avoid contact with the public, but the result was that there was a lack of active popular support for European integration. The mass of French people remained indifferent to this, as well as to other aspects of MRP foreign policy. This lack of support was reflected in the people's representatives in parliament. It is true that Robert Schuman had considerable justification for his stand that the executive must be free to negotiate international agreements. But he forgot one of the principles incorporated by Bidault in MRP policy: "Government is conciliation." It was seldom that Schuman tried to conciliate parliament.

An Article of Faith

The various criticisms that have been brought against MRP tactics constitute in part, at least, an indictment of France more than of the MRP. It has been hard for France and the intellectually divisive French to find that faith or conviction on issues that is necessary for almost all profound reform. The program of European integration, which was identified with the MRP, required a degree of devotion to the cause that was more easily developed by practicing Catholics than by *non-chrétien* French leaders. The members of the MRP had a high degree of unity and cohesion, politically as well as religiously. The vitriolic-tongued Domenach was forced to concede that Christian democrats were tied to the Mouvement by an "adhesion of the heart," having a religious veneration of their chiefs such as children often have of their parents.

The construction of Europe became a sort of "article of faith" for the MRP. "Absence of doctrine and failure of authority are directly connected," said Borne in *Terre Humaine* in 1953. There had been in the recent past, he thought, too many opinions and too few doctrines, one of which was the "European idea." Periodically, the MRP reminded France of the party's close association with European integration. At the Nantes Congress of 1950, the MRP sought to create an impression of indispensability through a motto affixed to the wall of the meeting room: "If France were to rebuild itself without the MRP, Europe would have to be constructed without France." But the party often resorted to faith instead of deeds. In contrast to pre-Reformation Catholics, it sought "justification through faith" rather than through works.

The MRP was continually preoccupied with European integration and, by 1954, was in danger of developing an obsession with the EDC, despite its earlier hesitations and equivocation. The same flat stand was taken publicly on other parts of the program of integration. In late 1951, Schuman maintained that failure to ratify the ECSC would call into question the whole French policy since the war. MRP leaders, who had cast scorn on the inflexibility of Communist doctrine, were themselves subject to the same charge of inflexibility in their policy of European integration.

The party made too much of the argument that there was no alternative to the EDC. In 1950, Scherer, speaking for the MRP parliamentary group, declared that if this Europe were not made, there would be a German Europe under the dominance of Russia. During the debate of February, 1952, Schuman told the Assembly that German membership in NATO as an alternative to the EDC would make the former look aggressive to Russian eyes because of the German territorial claims. By 1954, Alfred Coste-Floret's argument was that Russia would not have agreed to the impending Geneva meeting if the EDC had not been threatening; Maurice Schumann warned that the failure of the Treaty would result in the acceptance of anything by the French to escape diplomatic isolation; and Teitgen declared that the alternatives would be the gradual breakup of NATO and a rebirth of a popular front in France or the retreat of the latter into diplomatic isolation.

When the MRP members of the Government said there was no acceptable alternative, did they themselves really believe it? In their tactics, especially in early 1954, they overstressed this argument. It is unrealistic to assume the absence of an alternative to any move in foreign policy. As Aron has said, "Had the EDC partisans said, 'There is another solution,' and not 'This is the only solution,' the Assembly might have chosen the EDC."

Even the MRP *dirigeants* began to realize this. At the Lille Congress, Lecanuet, attempting to leave a door open in case of the failure of the EDC Treaty, said that the MRP did not hold to the superstition of a single chance for Europe. Borne had anticipated Lecanuet in this line of argument on the first day of the Congress; one objective, he said, should not turn the MRP away from others. As a matter of fact, it was only a matter of months after the EDC was finally defeated under Mendès-France in August, 1954, that an alternative was worked out through the expansion of the Brussels Pact, however successful or unsuccessful it may prove to be. To every course of action there is always an alternative.

The initial momentum and dynamism of the MRP had been almost exhausted by the end of 1952. Unfortunately, it was at this time that they were most needed to push toward a decision on the most critical plan, the EDC. It is ironic that the key to the compromises at home and in North Africa that had sapped the MRP's energies lay in the party's predominant foreign policies: resistance in Indochina and integration of Europe. The MRP had staked its prestige on policies for which French public opinion was not ready. It is, however, to the final credit of the MRP that, when the party found its program could not be achieved, it did not reverse its positions like the Radical Socialists to retain a place in the Government, but went instead into the opposition.[28]

9

Conclusions—In Retrospect and Prospect

The major obstacle to MRP success in foreign policy lay in the contradictory nature of its political philosophy. As a matter of fact, the party's emphasis on political philosophy was in itself a handicap. The French are famous for their intellectual independence, but in daily life and in everyday politics, they are quite a practical people. More than once, the writer heard comments adverse to the MRP because of its emphasis on a political philosophy that verged very closely on ideology. A resident of Burgundy (the one area that gave the MRP no votes in 1946) told the writer that his fellow Burgundians liked the MRP leaders as individuals but were afraid that they would *keep* their promises!

Various contradictions in this party philosophy provided particular stumbling blocks for the MRP. Profession and practice were frequently at odds. The party professed to be a movement; yet it was distinctly regional, and its direct influence was confined to a portion of the practicing Catholics and to a particular social level equivalent roughly to the lower middle class. It was not even able to reconcile the split between Left and Right in the Catholic Church, as it moved slowly to the Right.

The MRP had numerous Catholic or quasi-Catholic allies but none of great strength. Otherwise, its loss of the support of business, labor, the press, and the bureaucracy was significant, since effective foreign policy pressure groups were to be found in some of these fields. There was, therefore, little chance for the MRP to develop in practice the pluralism that was part of its political philosophy. As a movement, it expected to rally to its support as many groups—otherwise called natural communities—as possible. In fact, the family and the Church were the only two natural groups from which the party could get real support. But the French family as such is uninterested in foreign policy, and, on the other hand, the French Catholic Church had been in the past too international in approach.

148

With respect to the particular foreign policy objectives of the MRP, pluralism may well have been reflected in the functionalism of the Schuman Plan but not in the federalistic plan of a European Political Community. Pluralism was especially absent from party policy toward the French Union and North Africa, where centralization, rather than division of power, was the objective. Nor was pluralism to be found in the centralized structure of the party itself. Another contradiction in political philosophy was the contrast between the MRP's emphasis on economic internationalism and on human values and on the other hand, the party's preference for the *status quo* in North Africa or its opposition to the form of economic integration incorporated in the Strasbourg Plan.

Contradictions and confusion also existed in the MRP leadership; the words of the leaders were frequently at odds with their deeds. One reason for this may have been that the MRP was old at its birth. That is, in exterior parties like the MRP, the militants tend to predominate over the parliamentarians in party circles for some time. But the MRP Statutes insured predominance of the latter, and this in turn led to an increasing variance between the words of party doctrine (always dear to militants) and the deeds of parliamentarians. Moreover, there was serious disagreement between party leaders over priorities to be attached to party policies on European integration, on the East-West struggle, and on relations with the French Union and North Africa. Party leaders admitted to confusion over what the exact relationships should be between the European communities and the French Union or North Africa. Differences of opinion existed as well over the relationships between NATO and the EDC, over the political scope of the EPC, and over the eventual status of the Saar. With so many areas of disagreement, it is not surprising that party leaders, and especially those in the Government, involved themselves in frequent contradictions in their public statements.

More important even than these evidences of confusion were specific weaknesses of particular MRP leaders, for personalities have an important effect upon politics. Many of them lacked the degree of political skill necessary to cope with the troublesome French parliament. Even more serious was Schuman's disregard for the sensibilities of parliament and the failure of most party leaders to cultivate public opinion. The former was significant when one considers the important part assigned to common assemblies in the MRP program for the creation of European communities. The latter resulted from the disinclination of the party leaders to sponsor local civic activity. But the indictment, if any, might be brought against France, rather than against the party. The French are not very civic minded, and a tradition of resistance to government has developed. It would have been hard then, in any event, for the MRP to have stimulated popular support for a program of European integration.

The party leaders, who had to carry the ball for integration, appeared to fluctuate between excessive optimism for the chances of the communities, and a surprising lack of enthusiasm for certain plans such as Pflimlin's. This fluctuation was one aspect of the dualisms that existed within the MRP. Another was that the policy of the party Congresses conflicted with that of party leaders. And the emphasis on foreign policy by these leaders conflicted with the disregard for it in the lower echelons of the party—a crucial conflict, since this latter dualism existed despite the fact that, by 1950, European integration was almost the *raison d'être* of the MRP.

The Roadblock of Sovereignty

The MRP had enough difficulties within itself. One cannot forget, however, that it tried to accomplish its objectives among nationalistic, anticlerical French who were also jealous of their independence of American influence. The French preoccupation with sovereignty was the particular roadblock which barred the inclusion of a significant degree of pluralism in European institutions such as the ECSC and the EDC. Some MRP leaders other than Bidault were unrealistic in their disregard for this preoccupation with sovereignty. The demands of sovereignty also gave priority to the world role of France at the expense of its part in European integration. In this European program of the MRP, moreover, the anticlericals saw the danger of a "black Europe" under control of the Vatican. The growing social Catholicism of the MRP lent some basis to this criticism. And finally, the consistent, although not subservient, support given by the MRP to the foreign policy of the United States earned the party the unenvied nickname of the "American party."

Relative Success of the MRP

Let us now examine the positive contributions the MRP made to French foreign policy, despite all the above handicaps. By holding the foreign office for ten years, the party gave France a high degree of continuity in foreign policy. Much criticism has been leveled at the apparent fluctuations in recent American foreign policy. In contrast, from 1944 to 1954, one knew pretty well what France stood for in foreign affairs. A secondary but important result of this was that, even though the MRP was weakened by a lack of attention to foreign policy within its ranks, this foreign policy became an increasing factor, especially after 1953, in the rise and fall of French governments.

France is a country of many parties; it is quite a credit to a minor political party to survive for long in control of some part of the government in such a situation. Toward the end of the Fourth Republic, Mollet was complimented for having beaten the postwar record by holding on to the premiership for more than a year. France's parliament of the Fourth Republic could have driven many a statesman to distraction. The futility of the finely pointed arguments and the emotional clashes stood out as the author observed the National Assembly in action. Any party that could survive parliamentary attacks for as long as ten years deserves considerable credit. And the MRP's support of coalition governments may have saved France from the control of extremists like the Communists or the Gaullists.

With respect to its primary objective, although the MRP was not very successful in its entire program of European integration, it pushed through the important first step of a coal and steel community. Moreover, it was realistic in seeking such a practical area for integration. In preserving the idea of integration, throughout the difficult years thereafter and in the face of all the obstacles, the party made a significant contribution to the new giant step evident in the development of the European Common Market. In the discussions in the press, at the time of the creation of this European Economic Community, reference was sometimes made to the Schuman Plan as such, but not enough credit was given to the MRP for its dogged perseverance in paving the way.

The MRP also played an important part in obtaining the relative success of its second objective: to maintain a bridge between the East and West after the beginning of the Cold War in 1947. We are apt to forget how blunt the East-West break was in the years of the Korean conflict and how few political parties sought to maintain contact between East and West. This was a highly realistic policy for the MRP to follow in the context of French politics. And yet, we must remember that this policy of mediation and conciliation conflicted at various points with the party theory that peace is indivisible, since this theory often appeared to require resistance rather than negotiation. Even though it was a matter of party ideology rather than party practice, considerable political courage was needed for the development of a world strategy based on the MRP idea that peace is indivisible, and that France should not try to choose among its several critical problems. The party considered as opportunistic the thesis of Mendès-France that to govern is to choose, and believed that such a policy would merely postpone the day of reckoning for France.

The party opposed any extreme stands in its policy toward the East-West conflict. Just as it served as a neutralizer in internal politics, the MRP also tried to neutralize extreme tendencies in American foreign policy. It opposed a crusade against Communism at the same time that it opposed bargains between France and Russia. In general, it appears that the MRP favored conciliation rather than compromise in its foreign policy.

It was just as realistic for the MRP leaders to attempt conciliation between East and West as it was for them to support coalition government in France. If a valid distinction has been made between conciliation and compromise, from the French standpoint, the former was the better means of accommodation to employ. There were those like De Gaulle, who argued that France should conduct bilateral negotiations with Russia, since France was the only Western power (until 1952) that had a treaty with Russia. The trouble was that, in order to have such a negotiation or any sort of compromise, each side must have something that the other wants. In view of the fact that the MRP was committed to maintaining the world role of France and preserving the *status quo* in North Africa and Indochina, there was little that France (and its MRP Minister of Foreign Affairs) could offer Russia as a *quid pro quo* for Russian concessions, such as reduction of military forces. Would it be an abandonment of the program of European integration? But that was the keystone of MRP foreign policy. Through conciliation, however, time might be gained until world tension eased. The MRP could not take a rabid stand against Communism, for within France the Communists had considerable political strength, there was widespread opposition to a crusade against Communism, and MRP doctrine opposed capitalism as well as Communism. France, and the MRP within France, were in middle positions, which made mediation and conciliation logical policies.

Throughout all this difficult period, with such a complicated program, the degree of loyalty within the party to the demands of its foreign policy was quite unusual for French politics. On the face of things, despite under-the-surface disagreements among the leaders, the MRP was successful in its attempt to develop a non-Marxian centralized party in France. As a matter of fact, after having met over twenty leaders of the party, the author found evidence of a degree of integrity and courage among some of them and a unity that is unusual within any party.

Party Weaknesses

Because the MRP attempted conciliation in its domestic as well as in its foreign policy, it often fell into the quicksand of French internal politics and was forced to engage in various compromises for its own preservation. This carried over into at least one phase of party foreign policy, although as the MRP might have put it, the compromises were on nonessentials, to preserve the essential policy of European integration. In its relations with the North African protectorates, the MRP was very submissive to pressure groups and engaged in various compromises. Usually, one would think that close contacts with business would lead toward such submission to business pressure groups. But in the case of the MRP, it might well have been that the submission resulted from the lack of contact of its leaders with business and the resultant unfamiliarity with its propaganda techniques. In North Africa, the MRP demonstrated a flexibility toward pressure groups at the same time as it reflected rigidity toward the growing nationalism of the peoples there. There was also little flexibility in the MRP

policy of resistance in Indochina; at least, it was too rigid for a
French public opinion that was not ready for the sacrifices required
by such a policy as the MRP's.

In its principal program of European integration, the party was
also at least tactically unwise in its inflexibility. The MRP tried
unsuccessfully to persuade the French that there was no alternative
to the EDC. As a matter of fact, at least one alternative was found
in an expanded Western European Union only months after the
party had lost control of the foreign office. European integration
had become a sort of article of faith with the MRP. But it was unrealistic for the party to argue that there were no alternatives. And
in the larger sense, it was unrealistic for the MRP to argue that
France should not choose among European integration, the French
Union, and North Africa. Everything could not be done at once.
The party itself had proved this in choosing between contradictory parts of its political philosophy in developing its policy toward Indochina, North Africa, and, to a certain extent, European
integration. The inflexibility of the MRP approach was demonstrated once again in late 1954. Mendès-France was anathema to
some of the strongest party leaders and they were fighting him as
well as the Paris Pacts for an expanded Western European Union,
which he was sponsoring.

The MRP, whose Christian-democratic members were moving
slowly toward social Catholicism, was tied too much to the nineteenth century to lead such a secular state as France into a European community characterized by moral, economic, and political
integration. Either this European community would be too closely
related to Catholicism in the minds of the secular French, or else
it would demand an elasticity of approach that was foreign to the
conservatism typical of social Catholicism. In another sense, the
MRP was doomed to failure in its singlehanded attempt to lead
such a nationalistic state as France (the state of Bodin, of Louis
XIV, and of Clemenceau) into this supranational European community, which would be out of line with the nationalism typical
at least of the first half of the twentieth century.

Epilogue

Because of the MRP's continuous participation in the Government from 1944 to 1954, that period was clearly its heyday for influencing French foreign policy. The question arises, however, whether it is still enough of a force in French politics to influence foreign policy to any appreciable degree. In an effort to deal with this question, we shall first look at the MRP from the outside, examining its relative political success from 1954 to 1961 and its standing in the eyes of certain specialists in French politics. Thereafter, we shall seek to determine MRP goals in the areas of European, African, United Nations, and world policy by drawing upon National Congress reports and special reports of party *dirigeants* covering the same period.

It was in 1955 that a new Left was forming around the MRP bête noire, Mendès-France, including some former party allies such as the journal *Témoignage Chrétien*. Consequently, some MRP candidates in the 1956 elections sought shelter under other labels, but, in general, the party survived the elections much better than its leaders had anticipated. A total party vote of 2.4 million on the first ballot was reduced to 1.4 million on the second ballot. True, the MRP secured over 25 per cent of the vote in only three departments (and over 30 per cent only in Haut-Rhin and Bas-Rhin), but it had candidates in all but three of the metropolitan departments. It retained enough seats in the National Assembly to be fourth in strength in a political system which consisted of at least six principal parties. It was in 1956, according to Domenach, that the demise of the French Left began, with Mollet, the Socialist Premier, capitulating to the demands of the French *colons* in Algiers and with the Communists losing votes and their grip on labor, although winning seats in the Assembly.

It was the same political nightmare in Algeria that split the MRP. Their long-standing leader Bidault created a splinter group, Démocratie Chrétienne Française (French Christian Democrats),

155

and went on, in 1959, to organize a Rassemblement pour l'Algérie Française. He was banned from Algeria the following January, and disappeared from public sight in 1962, becoming a hunted man. On the other political wing, some Left Catholics left the MRP to join the Union de la Gauche Socialiste, led by Mendès-France. Pflimlin, however, received considerable Leftist support during his brief stand as Premier in the May, 1958, twilight of the Fourth Republic.

In 1958, the MRP won 35 councilor seats and gained 11 per cent of the total vote, compared to 9 per cent in 1951. Simonnet, Secretary-General, reminded the special National Congress of February, 1959, that since 1945, the party had regularly polled 2.5 million votes in first ballots for the Assembly, and had had continuous representation from 26 departments. It had been the only old party to gain in the elections of 1958, and the only "worker" in the Government was a member of the MRP. However, on the debit side of the ledger, the MRP was only present as a political force in 65 departments, had no deputies in the Assembly from the 8 largest cities, and only 8 deputies from cities with a population of more than 100,000.

Forewarned by these statistics, party members prepared for the municipal elections of March, 1959. Gaining representation in 21 of 25 cities with a population of over 100,000, the MRP increased its number of councilors from 110 to 150 (15 per cent of the total). In the senatorial elections of the same year, an increase from 28 to 36 senators represented the strongest advance of any party group, with the MRP holding as many seats as the amalgam party, Union of the New Republic. Half of the MRP senators were new, with farmers predominating. In the National Assembly, compared to 210 deputies of the UNR and 120 Independents, the MRP had 57, and had created a new parliamentary group *des Républicains Populaires et du Centre démocratique*.

Assuming its relative success in electoral battles, what role was the MRP to play in the new Fifth Republic? In the words of Leites, the days of the Fourth were those of multiple responsibility (which is as good as none), of relinquishment of real power to bureaucratic subordinates, of *immobilisme* and temporizing, and finally, of "government by catastrophe," with progress equivalent to that of a "dead leaf pushed by the wind."

In contrast, there is more centralization of responsibility under the Fifth. Poher, President of the MRP senatorial group, emphasized that the center of gravity has moved from the Left Bank of the Seine (where the parliament building is located) to the Right Bank (with its executive residence). But it is still a government of "technocrats" (despite De Gaulle's earlier antipathy toward them), with complicated patterns of decision-making in the cabinet and fuzzy ministerial functions, such as those of MRP's Lecourt, Minister of State for Community Affairs. As party President Pflimlin sees it, the two main dangers in the Fifth are technocracy, with precipitate action following upon secret preparations, and a tendency toward extremes, which would foster a spirit of violence and sap individual liberties.

In the eyes of specialists on French politics, what part could the MRP play in this new political drama? Prior to the transition to the Fifth, Morazé suggested that it might become the new Center. What Schoenbrun had called the "fratricidal war" with the Socialists had been tempered in 1955 by a renewed alliance. But, as Morazé put it, the "right to power" has been denied consistently in France to advocates of religious education. Moreover, one heavy obligation of a Center party is to change its opinions according to circumstances. Of course, we have seen that some *double-pensant* MRP leaders had had ample experience in this technique. And the party had not been free of equivocation. In fact, in 1961, a letter to the editor of the quasi party organ *France Forum* demanded less attention by MRP leaders to ideological vagaries and more attention to concrete objectives. It is the author's observation, however, that statements of party leaders such as Lecanuet have become less verbose and more specific in some recent instances.

Among Morazé's criticisms of the past tactics of the MRP, were that its leaders had not properly prepared valid technical data for the European Defense Community, and, in the final stages, cosignatories of the treaty "were given three days to accept modifications France had taken three years to formulate." Leites, in his turn, found the MRP emphasis emotional rather than intellectual. It had temporized and equivocated, had put opponents like Mendès-France into power to accomplish painful tasks and thereby ruin themselves. Its party pronouncement on Algeria in 1957, said

Leites, was too vague; the following spring, Pflimlin first acted
boldly, then backslid, preferring a "contest between rates of de-
cay" in the Algerian crisis.

There are some like Yates who believe that the MRP's continued
retention of the title Mouvement is more egoistic than realistic.
But the party is reluctant to abandon this claim, and in actuality
there is a need for something like a movement in French politics.
Williams has noted that the MRP, "a mushroom party," first
established itself through local organizations. Not so the UNR of
the Fifth, which was organized from the top and reflected extremist tendencies that would endanger the chances for vital political
life in France. The implication is that, should the MRP seek to
stimulate local political life, its value to France as well as its own
political stock would rise.

Recurring time and again in the comments of specialists on
French politics is the observation of the lack of *civisme* among
the French, who have come to look on themselves as subjects
rather than as citizens participating in government. Schoenbrun
associated this lack of *civisme* with the long tradition of French
code law. Moreover, during the Fourth Republic, all political
opinion was centered in a parliament whose structure was designed
to prevent action, which left the job of preserving political continuity to the administrators (*fonctionnaires*).

The need for a movement has been even more evident under
the Fifth. In reports to the MRP in 1960 and 1961, Lecanuet de-
plored the increasing indifference to political life. Although the
choices made by De Gaulle in French foreign policy are so crucial
for France and for the West, the people have little say about them.
Unconditional "yes" or "no" answers on referendums are no true
reflection of democracy. Administrators and technocrats are gov-
erning, and there is no dialogue between the people and the power.

However, the MRP does not want a return to the pattern of the
Fourth, and little chance is seen for a swing to the American
Presidential system of government. In the eyes of the budding
leader of the MRP Lecanuet, the irreplaceable party mission is to
save France from civil war. True patriotism does not lie in a policy
of force, said Lecanuet (perhaps thinking of Bidault's tendency),
but in cooperation in the evolution of new forms while preserving
essentials. Optimism could be found, at least, in the demographic

transformation of France into a young nation, a process in accord with a primary MRP goal, development of the family. But most essential is the search for new avenues of political debate, through professions, labor organizations, and private associations. It is true that in the past French parties have had no significant educational influence on their electorates; only the Communists have "educated" their electors. As Brogan said, there seems to be no democratic assumption in France of a contractual relationship between electors and elected. The latter pay more attention, in national and international policy, to interest groups than to their constituents.

A growing awareness appeared in the MRP National Congresses of 1956 and 1957 of past inadequacies in making contacts with the French citizenry. Not until the special National Congress of February, 1959, were detailed plans considered for implementing this goal. Simonnet, Secretary-General, reminded the assemblage that it was a proper function of political parties to keep the public informed. "Men pass," he said, perhaps thinking of De Gaulle, and it is clearly a duty of the MRP to develop public opinion in order to preserve democracy; no true democracy exists without political debates. Both Simonnet and Pflimlin referred to the need for a dialogue between the State and the people.

The MRP continued to distribute the biweekly *Forces Nouvelles* until recently and for two years has supported a magazine of political opinion, *France Forum*. But more is needed; it is necessary to start at the commune, the "primary school of politics." Now that less time is spent preparing for elections, more can be done, said Simonnet, especially in this fluid political epoch when three-fourths of the deputies in the National Assembly are new. But time is of the essence; if something constructive is not done, the abdication of their responsibilities by the citizens could be once again a forerunner of fascism.

What steps has the party actually taken toward this goal? A Commission Nationale de Formation Politique has been created, and at the special Congress of February, 1959, a statutory National Bureau was planned, to be chosen either by the Congress or the National Committee and to act on behalf of the MRP in contacting kindred groups. In recreating an "open movement," MRP *dirigeants* specifically wanted liaison with a new national committee for *rassemblement des forces démocratiques,* which had contacted the MRP President the previous month. By 1961, a Study Commission for the Future of Democracy had been organized by the MRP.

In the earlier words of Bidault, who ironically had removed himself from the party, the MRP hoped again to be the "party of tomorrow." It sought to contact youth both in the *métropole* and *outre-mer* (with fingers crossed, party leaders noted that almost half the Algerians were under twenty). But although making contact with the *rassemblement,* the MRP did not want to be a party *mi-politique, mi-syndicaliste,* like the British Labour Party. Nor, despite any new liaisons, did it want to change its name.

With respect to general party goals, President Pflimlin indicated that the MRP did not base its plans on crises (referring to De Gaulle's pattern). It sought to develop the legislative role of parliament. Pflimlin said that he would like to see a parliamentary regime *à l'anglaise* in France. Having in mind, perhaps, the frenetic chauvinism in some of the Assembly debates of the Fourth, he also said that one of the main dangers of the Fifth was nationalism. A major aim of the MRP was to preserve the distinction between patriotism and nationalism. Wise patriotism, said Pflimlin, would allow for such international policies as European integration.

We come now to the recent stands taken by the MRP on French foreign-policy issues. Its present political standing and tendencies discussed above are an integral part of its potential effect on foreign policy. For the party has to maintain its electoral strength, looking toward the day when individuals pass, and it has to widen its contacts in French political life to overcome a principal weakness of its structure from 1944 to 1954.

The MRP has had at least its share of equivocation and impreciseness in foreign policy. Now that it is free of compromising ties with the Government, how precise has it become? For an answer, we turn to pronouncements of party leaders in this centralized party (Schoenbrun used the word *monolithic;* the author was prevailed upon to use the softer word in his original study of the base period, 1944–1954). As Simonnet said in 1959, the party is democratic in its support of free discussion, but once a decision is taken, it is to be applied by all. The reader will remember that this is the same Simonnet who headed the Commission that read Denis out of the party for his opposition to the EDC.

The reports of *dirigeants* that follow, for the period 1956 to 1961, are those of the elder statesman Robert Schuman, the former Secretary-General Colin, the North African specialist Le Brun Kéris, the party President Pflimlin, the chairmen of the senatorial and assembly party groups, Poher and Bosson, and the budding leader Lecanuet (all of whom the author either personally interviewed or heard speak in 1954). Also we hear from the longstanding party spokesman Maurice Schumann, and from more recent figures, such as Mendette and Aguesse.

European Policy

At a time when De Gaulle has clearly indicated his belief that European integration has had its day, the "European party" is laboring under a temporary handicap. Yet it has not faltered in its objective. After having been honored in 1958 with the first Presidency of the Common Assembly for the Common Market and Euratom, Robert Schuman strongly supported quick ratification of the treaty creating the former and announced adhesion of the MRP to Monnet's committee for a United States of Europe. At the Congresses of 1960 and 1961, the MRP continued to aim for a political Europe with a common foreign policy and with a structure embracing periodic meetings of heads of the member governments, a permanent secretariat, election by universal suffrage of delegates to a European Assembly, and creation of a European University. These goals were so significant to the MRP that in May, 1962, five MRP members of De Gaulle's cabinet resigned in protest against the latter's public scorn cast upon the idea of European federalism. These five were Pflimlin (Minister of State for Cooperation with African States), Maurice Schumann (Minister for Economic Development), Buron (Minister of Public Works and Transport), Bacon (Minister of Labor), and Fontanet (Public Health Minister).

Since, however, the MRP had first sought an economic Europe, rather than one of "strategies," it noted with pleasure how the Common Market had flourished, entering its third stage of tariff reductions in January, 1961, and finally agreeing a year later on a common agricultural policy, which MRP specialist Charpentier had been working toward for years. The MRP favored the development of a common external tariff for an expanded European Economic Community to include Great Britain and the other members of the "Outer Seven." Poher became precise on domestic agricultural policy in announcing that the MRP sought commercialization of French agriculture and concentration on animal production.

In emphasizing the importance of Western solidarity, party leaders said that France could not expect this if it was not willing to enter into healthy integration rather than rely on a policy of national prestige. But it should speak frankly to the United States and insist on the right to nuclear arms, which would be an assistance to NATO, which, in turn, would help integration. France must not always be the *gendarme à pied* on the Continent. The MRP also supported U.S. installation of missile bases in Europe.

Already in 1959, Maurice Schumann had been dealing with the primary threat to the peace implicit in the status of Berlin. The man who had been the principal radio voice of the French Resistance in Great Britain during World War II said that he would remain "faithful to his youth" and that France must not forget it had Czechoslovakia on its conscience. "Will there be new Marcel Déat's?" he asked. ("I will not die for Danzig.") The West had stood firm at Quemoy and Beirut, and so it must at Berlin; the guarantee of NATO was at stake. The West must avoid changing the status of Berlin, even condoning a U.N. guarantee of all Berlin which might lead to asphyxia for the Western segment. It must oppose manifestations of neutralism such as would be reflected in the "disengagement" zone contemplated in the Rapacki Plan.

What was needed, rather, was political disengagement. Should the West weaken on Berlin, it would dishearten the satellite peoples and lead to more "anti-Westism" among them. Khrushchev was raising the German bogey as a matter of tactics; in MRP eyes, a Christian Democratic Germany was quite different from the old one (no particular thought was given to how long the Christian Democrats might stay in power).

However, while keeping its bargaining points secret, the West should be ready for conciliation and should understand Russia's bitter memories. It should accept the challenge of economic competition implicit in a policy of coexistence, and should create in Europe a market for underdeveloped areas.

Central to the MRP approach to European policy, was an assumption that Mendette made explicit, the assumption that time is working for the West. When one remembers that MRP leaders thought time was working for the EDC, one is troubled. There is much doubt on this question; but we should not discount too quickly and pessimistically such an approach to world issues.

African Policy

Characteristic of MRP policy toward Africa in these recent years, has been a concern for preserving French economic stakes and for protecting the Continent from Communism. A Eur-African association would prevent Khrushchev from turning the flank of the West. This preference for association over assimilation was made clear by Colin in 1957, as he admitted that the latter pleased neither Africa nor the *métropole*. Complete independence, on the other hand, was seen as a precursor of another colonization by Communism. Yet the 1957 Congress resolutions were vague; there was still a preoccupation with French investments. Some improvement was visible in the report of Le Brun Kéris the following year. To help the Africans help themselves, investments should be maintained, but through bilateral negotiations with specific areas rather than through the antiquated FIDES plan of 1946. The French Community should be built, not just defined.

It was in 1958 also that the MRP stood firm for inclusion, in the Treaty of Rome for a Common Market, of a provision for a fund for investments in France Overseas. As a result, economic exchange between French Africa and the European Economic Community had increased by 50 per cent, with $320 million disbursed through the fund by 1961. In that year, a Strasbourg resolution of the European Assembly supported a new association, open to all Africa, the primary goal of which was to raise the standard of living, with secondary goals of substitution of a moderate preferential system for direct aid from Europe and stimulation for diversification of crops. Mallet of the MRP gave the impression that the party favored this development. Poher had previously suggested that such budding African leaders as Senghor (former MRP member and now President of Senegal) need not worry about "balkanization," since an African common market was already being contemplated and was supported by another former MRP adherent, Maga, now President of Dahomey.

The MRP took pride in the fact that in 1955 its *dirigeant* Teitgen had proposed the *loi-cadre* that established the framework for African participation in political affairs in France Overseas. It also claimed (somewhat dubiously, in the light of MRP equivocations) that De Gaulle had chosen the same path for Algeria that the party had long supported.

The 1957 pronouncements of former party Secretary-General Colin on Algeria seemed still to have a backward rather than a forward look. What was needed, he said, was maintenance of French security zones, development of a federalist structure, but above all firmness, which the Moslems were supposed to respect. The suggestions of the African specialist, Le Brun Kéris, the following year, were more constructive. Councils presided over by Africans should be made responsible to African assemblies, and a new cadre of French administrators, teamed with some Africans, should be developed. Internal autonomy should be completed and African territories grouped together in the interests of efficiency. France should accept international assistance in building French Africa, but internationalization as such was no panacea. With respect to Algeria, he and other *dirigeants* opposed both the use of force and, on the other hand, the abandonment of Algeria, admitting that France must accept the risks of a democratic choice there. But strategic bases must be maintained, as well as a hold on the Sahara (France's "future daily bread"), and the nationality rights of the *colons* must be preserved. Nonetheless, there was a need not just to talk, but to act; "intellectual constructions" were no better than their execution.

Lecanuet reflected this approach in 1961, when he said that "auto-determination" was the solution in this tinderbox of North Africa. Upon such a peaceful solution, depended the future of liberty in France. The longer the war lasted, the more Communism could penetrate Africa. There should, however, certainly be a guarantee of protection to the French minority in Algeria, without which there could not be the essence of democracy in practice. It was the search for a solution in Algeria, he said, that justified the presence of MRP members in the Government. Of course, they were thereby taking their chances with the OAS. As a matter of fact, in January, 1962, a *plastic* bomb was exploded in the home of Paul Coste-Floret in Montpellier.

United Nations Policy

In its attitude toward the United Nations, the MRP had for a long time taken an "orthodox" position in France, insisting, for example, that the U.N. should not interfere in domestic problems in Morocco—and then in Tunisia—and now in Algeria. Between 1956 and 1959, party leaders had become increasingly bitter, charging that nations within the U.N. that had no respect for freedom condemned those like France that believed in the rights of man. It appeared that sanctions were sought only against those nations that would accept them (in the light of the Suez and Hungary affairs). It is interesting that Le Brun Kéris, in identifying the U.N. as a docile servant of new imperialisms, was referring not just to Egypt but to India, which he claimed was stretching its tentacles out to such areas as Madagascar (a penetrating thinker, Le Brun Kéris apparently had anticipated the Goa incident).

Despite its criticisms, the MRP opposed French separation from the U.N. On the contrary, Aguesse argued that since U.N. members were obliged to refrain from aggression, it was rather redundant to enter pacts renouncing the use of nuclear weapons. In fact, he said that a halt in testing would increase the present international disequilibrium (thinking, no doubt, of France's relative position) were it not accompanied by a pact for general disarmament. Aguesse seems rather illogical to equate the renunciation of nuclear weapons with an obligation to refrain from aggression; 50 per cent, let us say, of the nuclear weapons would be used to repel aggression.

In 1961, Poher reminded the MRP Congress that the United Nations is a mirror of the world as it is and that refusal of France to participate would lead to isolation. It was significant, he said, that Khrushchev's attack on Hammarskjöld had not been sustained by the new nations, which wished to maintain the U.N. Despite opposition by the United States in the U.N. to British or French policies, it was well to seek to convince the U.S. of its need to state disagreements clearly but to preserve Western solidarity. Although American troops were still needed in Europe, U.S. opposition to France in Algeria and in developing atomic weapons impeded the "world reply" to Communism.

World Role

Both Colin in 1957 and Lecanuet in 1960 recalled the MRP doctrine that peace is indivisible; *tout est solidaire* in a universe where "nothing is isolated." So also, Pflimlin underlined the continuous party concern for conciliation. There must be a continual search for a dialogue.

A less complacent approach, however, is typical of recent MRP political philosophy. Although coexistence is the essence of Western civilization, Schumann emphasized that it is only a phase in Communist ideology in its demand for total victory. The recent *détente* (relaxation of tensions) was the result of Western unity, partly developed through the program of integration. But no longer were MRP leaders so assured that time worked in favor of the West. Rather, Russian power was growing, the satellites would become more hopeless of eventual liberation, and Russia would seek to disintegrate the West. Nor could the West yet draw much solace from incipient Russo-Chinese rivalry; it is not yet as significant as the dual complicity in opposing the West.

What, then, is the way out of the impasse? Perhaps, said Schumann, the *Tiers-Monde* might provide the means for a dialogue. The rise in the importance of underdeveloped nations is the significant development of this period in history. Already in 1959, the Bandung Conference had refused admittance to Russia. It should be MRP policy, he said, to support a "grand community" embracing this Third World, to be added to the French Community, NATO, and the European Community. The European Economic Community should aid the economically weak peoples of the world, and Russia should be invited to join in this task.

But not China, be it noted. Perhaps the MRP leadership was coming around, as were many others, to the approach that Russia and the West would soon have to team up against this colossus of the East. This is the very prediction made to the author, in 1954, by the leader of the Jeune République, on the Left wing of the MRP.

APPENDIX A

Interviews

Between April 6 and June 15, 1954, the author had the opportunity to interview twenty-two members of the MRP (most of them *dirigeants*), for periods ranging from half an hour to two hours. When the meetings had been arranged (which in some cases took considerable time), the author was always courteously and well received, and the general impression he obtained was that the leadership of the party was composed of men who were above average in political morality. The detailed criticisms in the body of this study have been made with humility and with full awareness of how many of such criticisms could be leveled as well at many other political parties.

Footnote references to Appendix A refer, then, to these interviews, as well as to personal attendance at the Lille Congress and in some very few instances, to investigations made during a trip by Fiat for 2,200 miles in a loop south of Paris. The writer prepared a detailed report of these interviews and investigations on the return sea voyage from France, and this in turn was based on notes taken at the interviews and expanded on the same day.

The following political figures were interviewed in France by the author at least once:

MRP	*Non-MRP*
Robert Schuman	R. Louis
Jacques Mallet	S. Cleveland
Maurice Farine	Leleu
Robert Bichet	Raymond Aron
G. Le Brun Kéris	Francisque Gay
Fontaneau	François Goguel
Leo Hamon	Bertrand Schneider
André Monteil	
Delfosse	
Lecourt	

MRP

Bosson
Janton
Fréville
Fontanet
Buron
Colin
Pflimlin
Poher
Borne
Poisson
Mme. Peyrolles
Delahoutre

The author personally attended speeches given by the following political figures:

MRP	*Non-MRP*
P. H. Teitgen	De Gasperi
H. Teitgen	Spaak
Vignes	Mollet
P. Coste-Floret	Hallstein
A. Coste-Floret	Laniel
Bouret	Lussy
Mme. Dupuis	Bardoux
Lecanuet	Denis (André)*
Max André	Daladier
Sauvage	Le Trocquer
Boudet	Pierre André
M. Schumann	Mounier
Georges Bidault	Lejeune
Bacon	Mendès-France
Prigent	
Bouxom	

* Already excluded from the MRP at the time.

Principal Leaders of the MRP

Reference has been made in the text to the background of some of the MRP leaders, and especially to that of Robert Schuman. Until he left the party in 1959, its other principal leader was Georges Bidault, whom Mauriac characterized in 1950 as the *fils spirituel* of Marc Sangnier. In his recent book, published during the Fourth Republic, Luethy called Bidault a "bold idealist, who has totally unjustifiably acquired the reputation of a small-scale Machiavelli." Yet Bidault is, to say the least, a complicated individual. With a diverse background of training in both Jesuit and lay schools, he taught history before he joined the Popular Democrats (PDP). He attacked Fascist and Nazi aggression as editor of *L'Aube* in the 1930's and became President of the National Council of the Resistance during the war. Representing the Center rather than the Left or Right wing of the MRP, Bidault was handicapped by a past that included his period of responsibility as foreign minister for carrying out De Gaulle's foreign policy in 1944 and 1945 and also his support for the later tense collaboration between the MRP and the Communists until 1947.

Bidault held the Ministry of Foreign Affairs from September, 1944, to July, 1948, and was chosen President of the MRP in 1949 to succeed Maurice Schumann. At this time, foreseeing the eventual decline of the RPF, Bidault maintained a tone of personal respect for De Gaulle as part of his plan of calculated moderation to bring back errant voters to the MRP. After his stint as Premier from October, 1949, to June, 1950, Bidault again returned to his position as a deputy in the National Assembly, but could not stay out of the Government for long. In early 1953, after holding other posts, he returned to the Ministry of Foreign Affairs and continued to hold it until Laniel was overthrown as Premier in June, 1954.

Among the MRP leadership in 1949, only Bidault, Schuman, De Menthon, Teitgen, and Letourneau were directly connected with formulating foreign policy. Sangnier, the originator of *Sillon*, died soon thereafter, and, by 1949, the earlier leader Francisque Gay had begun slowly and carefully to sever his contacts with the party. By 1954, other leaders included Maurice Schumann, a former party President who then was Secretary of State for Foreign Affairs, Lecourt as chairman of the parliamentary group, the intellectual Étienne Borne, Poher in the Council of the Republic, and Pierre Pflimlin, who recently has been President of the MRP.

De Menthon, a law professor from Haute-Savoie, was very active in the Constituent Assembly of 1945, was Vice-President and later President of the Consultative Assembly of the Council of Europe, and also, for a long time, was leader of the MRP group in the National Assembly. He is well respected, comes from a department where the party is well organized, and is a connecting link with the moderates in French politics. André Colin, a former leader of the ACJF, served for over ten years as Secretary-General of the party. From 1952 to 1956, the President of the party was Pierre-Henri Teitgen, who had been very active in the Resistance and subsequently became a deputy from Ille-et-Vilaine in Brittany and also a member of the Government.

Maurice Schumann, from the department Nord, has also been President of the party and has represented France in the United Nations, besides having been in the Government prior to June, 1954, and more recently, the chairman of the National Assembly's Committee on Foreign Affairs. More impressive perhaps in writing or over the radio than in person, Schumann was the voice of the Resistance on the London radio during the war and later, as editor of *L'Aube*, perpetuated the pattern that had been set in the 1930's by Bidault. Other party figures include the Coste-Floret twins and Lecanuet, a young deputy who first acted as *rapporteur* on foreign policy at the National Congress in 1954.

Separate mention should be made of Robert Buron, who was somewhat unorthodox in the stands that he took within the party; he had as close contacts with the business world as any party leader and was the only member of the MRP besides Monteil to enter the 1954 Mendès-France cabinet. Thereafter, he left the party, but later returned and until May, 1962, was serving in the Government as Minister of Public Works and Transport. He also helped negotiate the Evian Algerian cease-fire agreement. Reference has already been made above to Pierre Pflimlin. This Alsatian deputy has perhaps the brightest political future of any present leader of the MRP; he held the ministry of finance in the 1955 Faure cabinet, had the same position in the Gaillard cabinet, and thereafter served as the last Premier of the Fourth Republic.*

* Sources for this information, other than my interviews referred to in Appendix A, include the following items in the Bibliography: III, 1, 8; IV, 25; V, 17, 37, 44, 62, 67.

Notes

Chapter 1: Historical Background

1. *L'Aube*, May 20–21, 1950, p. 1.
2. *L'Aube*, May 29, 1950, p. 2; Mario Einaudi and François Goguel, *Christian Democracy in Italy and France*, p. 112.
3. A social Catholic suggested to the author in 1954 that the PRL (Parti Républicain de la Liberté) was the closest to his group of Catholics, but social Catholics do not tend to group in parties.
4. *Action Civique et Politique*, No. 16 (June, 1960), p. 27; No. 19 (May–June, 1961), p. 14.
5. For other sources used in this chapter and not referred to above, see the following items in the Bibliography: IV, 18; V, 20, 29, 32, 56, 67, 107; VI, 1, 2, 9, 14.

Chapter 2: Relation of Party Structure to Foreign Policy

1. See Appendix A. Goguel, a Protestant, seems able to take a relatively objective view of the MRP. See also *Esprit*, September, 1951, p. 364; *Journal of Modern History*, September, 1952, pp. 275–82.
2. *Revue Politique et Parlementaire*, November, 1953, pp. 248–57; *Terre Humaine*, July–August, 1952, pp. 76–99; *Vie Intellectuelle*, October, 1950, pp. 276–301; Herbert Luethy, *France Against Herself*, pp. 386–87, 426–27. This controversy lasted two years. "Robert Schuman a-t-il brûlé Jeanne d'Arc?" asked Borne at one point.
3. *Manchester Guardian Weekly*, February 21, 1952, p. 2; *L'Aube*, May 29, 1950, p. 1; May 30, 1950, p. 1; *Journal des Débats*, February 2, 1952, p. 631; *Nation*, July 18, 1953, p. 45; *New York Times*, January 29, 1954; *Figaro*, May 31, 1954, p. 5.
4. In voting on the EDC on August 30, 1954, the Socialists split 53 pro, 50 con. The EDC was rejected by a vote of 319 to 264. (*New York Times*, October 11, 1954, p. 1.) In a comment on the Pope's expression of regret at the rejection of the EDC, it was suggested in the non-Catholic *Christian Century* (January 26, 1955, p. 104) that the opposition by MRP deputies later in 1954 to the Paris Pacts for an expanded Western Union indicated that "the Catholic Party would support European unification so long as the union . . . promised to be Catholic-controlled."
5. Senator Hamon (MRP until 1954) has a Jewish background, and La Gravière and senator Walker were prominent Protestants. Mauriac agreed with Fauvet that the MRP was generally nonclerical. (François Mauriac, *Journal*, IV, 163.) Lecourt, parliamentary leader of the MRP *groupe* in 1954, said at that time that the party was more laic than it had been in 1945. He defined "laic" in such a way as to imply that the relations of Church and state were those of neutrality rather than conflict. (See Appendix A.)
6. *L'Aube*, September 5, 1950, p. 1.

7. Gordon Wright, *The Reshaping of French Democracy*, pp. 65–77.

8. Maurice Duverger, *Les Partis Politiques*, p. 12; Taylor Cole (ed.), *European Political Systems*, p. 662.

9. Duverger, *op. cit.*, pp. 8–33.

10. Ibid., pp. 8–16;*Manchester Guardian Weekly*, December 6, 1951, p. 3; *Figaro*, May 31, 1954, p. 5. But in August, 1954, they did not follow the requirements of the Congress.

11. See Appendix B for biographical material.

12. A careful study of the development of public opinion is not within the scope of this work. However, some public opinion polls referred to in *Sondages* indicated that in 1952, 55 per cent of those questioned favored participation in European integration and 59 per cent would accept participation in a European *government*. The following year, 65 per cent of those questioned favored a union of Western European countries for other than military purposes; only 13 per cent opposed it. By 1954, however, there was a more equal division of opinion over the related question of whether the German mentality had changed from the time of Hitler. At least, there appeared to be a basis for significant support for European integration in France, which the MRP did not do enough to nourish.

13. *Sic*. See Article 20 of the Statutes. Elsewhere, it is referred to as the Executive Commission. In interviews at the Secretariat, the author was unable to find that there were two separate bodies.

14. In the author's interview with Colin, the Secretary-General referred to another body, an inner Bureau. It was considered better, he said, to have an official inner clique than one growing out of personalities. Mallet, Secretariat official in charge of foreign policy matters, was unaware of the existence of this bureau.

15. The report of the Commission on Discipline is dated January 10, 1954. The author received a copy from the Secretariat. Simmonet was chosen Secretary-General of the MRP in 1956. (*New York Times*, January 13, 1956, p. 1.)

16. *Forces Nouvelles*, May 30, 1953, p. 1. See the report of Simmonet referred to in the Bibliography, and also the comment of Philip Williams in his article in *Occidente*, XI, No. 5 (1955), 377.

17. *L'Aube*, February 10–11, 1951, p. 6.

18. *Ibid.*, May 27–28, 1950, p. 1; *Terre Humaine*, June, 1952, p. 122; *L'Année Politique*, 1952, p. 37; Jacques Fauvet, *De Thorez à De Gaulle—Les Forces Politiques*, p. 170. "When one acts, one becomes slightly the traitor [to his ideals]."

19. *Journal des Débats*, November 20, 1953, pp. 5354 ff.

20. *Manchester Guardian Weekly*, March 6, 1952, p. 8; *L'Aube*, June 19, 1950, p. 4.

21. *Journal des Débats*, November 20, 1953, pp. 5354 ff.; *Terre Humaine*, June, 1952, p. 122; *L'Année Politique*, 1952, p. 38. But the motion adopted on the EDC in the Socialist Congress of 1952 was even vaguer than that in the MRP Congress. (*The Times* [London], May 31, 1952, p. 6.)

22. Einaudi and Goguel, *op. cit.*, pp. 204–5; Herbert Luethy, *France Against Herself*, p. 408.

23. For other sources used in this chapter and not referred to above, see the following items in the Bibliography: I, 5, 7, 15; III, 5, 8, 13; IV, 2, 3, 11, 14, 18, 22, 27, 34, 36, 41, 45; V, 3, 29, 32, 37, 41, 60, 88, 100, 106, 107; VI, 16.

Chapter 3: Allies and Adversaries

1. Hannah Arendt, *The Origins of Totalitarianism*, pp. 250–51.
2. See reference to this cleavage in *L'Aube*, May 20–21, 1950, p. 1.
3. Catholic youth groups (*Jeunesse Chrétienne*) connected with special occupations such as farming, education, the navy, etc.
4. *L'Aube*, June 20, 1950, p. 3; *New York Times*, September 14, 1952, p. 1; December 25, 1953, p. 1; December 27, 1953, Sect. IV, p. 5.
5. *Le Monde*, January 26, 1954, p. 5. See also Appendix A.
6. *L'Aube*, May 11, 1950, p. 3; *Manchester Guardian Weekly*, May 25, 1950, p. 8; June 22, 1950, p. 3; Dorothy Pickles, *French Politics*, p. 207; *Foreign Affairs*, April, 1953, p. 353; *Chroniques de Politique Étrangère*, July–September, 1950, p. 523.
7. *Esprit*, June, 1953, pp. 827–48; *Forces Nouvelles*, supplement to No. 53, January 2, 1954, pp. 22–23; *Terre Humaine*, June–July, 1953, pp. 108–13.
8. Gabriel Almond, *The Appeals of Communism*, p. 385.
9. At its Paris headquarters, the MRP also issued a journal for its militants, *MRP à l'Action*.
10. *Reporter*, September 16, 1952, p. 9.
11. *Esprit*, September, 1951, p. 375; *Terre Humaine*, September, 1951, pp. 14–19.
12. For other sources used in this chapter and not referred to above, see the following items in the Bibliography: I, 3; II, 5; III, 4, 13; IV, 11, 22; V, 3, 20, 37, 38, 55, 56, 76, 100, 107; VI, 1, 9.

Chapter 4: European Integration

1. Material based on an unpublished paper of the author which in turn was based on: Office of the High Commissioner for Germany, *9th Report on Germany*, p. 4; *The Economist*, July 5, 1952, p. 28; *International Organization*, August, 1952, pp. 464 ff.; *Commonweal*, March 21, 1952, p. 588.
2. See summary of the treaty in *New York Times*, May 28, 1952, p. 14.
3. This is very interesting in view of the number of "technocrats" who have participated in the government of De Gaulle's Fifth Republic.
4. Sigmund Neumann, *Modern Political Parties*, pp. 139–40.
5. But nonparty man Monnet worked out the details. According to one source, he was also the originator of the idea of an EDC. (*New York Times*, January 12, 1953, p. 6.)
6. Theodore H. White, *Fire in the Ashes*, pp. 261–62; *L'Aube*, May 30, 1950, p. 3; *Catholic World*, January, 1951, p. 250. For brief biographies of other leaders, see Appendix B.
7. *New York Times*, September 21, 1950, p. 5; October 26, 1950, p. 8.
8. To Pflimlin, there was only an ideological significance to the term "pluralism"—that is, it implied a mutual recognition of conflicting ideologies in a positive sort of coexistence. Borne understood pluralism to imply the "free confrontation" of all groups. (See Appendix A.)
9. *Le Monde*, January 14, 1954, p. 1; *Jeune Europe*, No. 23, pp. 7 ff.; *L'Aube*, January 15, 1951, p. 3.
10. *Journal des Débats*, November 17, 1953, pp. 5187–93; *New Yorker*, September 11, 1954, p. 80.
11. *Ouest France*, April 6, 1954, p. 1; *Journal des Débats*, February 12, 1952,

pp. 573–76; February 13, 1952, pp. 677–83, 695. Teitgen's reference to *croisades* was an unfortunate choice of words, since at the time the idea of a crusade to liberate Eastern Europe was particularly distasteful to the French. Bidault's reference to a "corner of land" appealed to the property-conscious French, ever fearful of losing some of their land to Germany again.

12. *Journal of Political Economy*, LXI (April, 1953), 169. Also see Appendix A. In view of Pflimlin's rising status in the party (by 1956, he had risen to be President), his opinion was likely to bear considerable weight. Nonetheless, Teitgen was insisting later in the year that the EPC be above the ECSC and EDC.

13. *L'Aube*, February 17–18, 1951, p. 3; *Nord-Éclair*, January 12, 1954, p. 1. Bidault later credited the Quai d'Orsay with a principal hand in the formulation of the policy of European integration. If that was true, the permanent officials there imposed, if anything, Rightist checks on the program. (*Le Monde*, April 24, 1954, p. 4.)

14. See the last section of Chapter VIII. It was the opinion of the political specialist Fauvet that the European Defense Community Treaty could have been ratified in 1952 and even in 1953. The MRP members mistakenly thought time was running in their favor. (Daniel Lerner and Raymond Aron, *France Defeats the EDC*, pp. 134–35.)

15. Luethy asked whether a new type of entrepreneur will spring up if it is accepted that the solution for economic troubles is European union. See *Occidente*, XI, No. 5 (1955), 414. But in the light of the effect of the Common Market on French industry, perhaps Luethy was too pessimistic.

16. *New York Times*, August 29, 1953, p. 4; March 21, 1954, p. 12.

17. With respect to the question of constitutionality, see: *Journal des Débats*, November 20, 1953, pp. 5363–65; p. 12 of a special pamphlet on Bidault's speech of that time; *New York Times*, February 20, 1954, p. 3; Mouvement Européen, *Douze Lettres sur la Communauté de Défense*, 1954, pp. 57–60.

18. *Forces Nouvelles*, May 30, 1953, p. 8; *L'Aube*, April 8–9, 1950, p. 1.

19. Mauriac, *op. cit.*, p. 42.

20. *L'Aube*, June 22, 1950, p. 3; November 16, 1950, p. 1; November 28, 1950, p. 3.

21. *The Times*, September 25, 1952, p. 4.

22. *New York Times*, September 27, 1953, p. 1; November 21, 1953, p. 1; *U.S. News and World Report*, November 20, 1953, p. 64.

23. *Forces Nouvelles*, May 31, 1952, pp. 8, 11, 12; May 30, 1953, p. 12.

24. *Occidente*, XI, No. 5 (1955), 369; *Terre Humaine*, September, 1952, p. 74.

25. *Nouvelles de l'Europe*, September–October, 1952, p. 9; *New York Times*, June 11, 1953, p. 1. Also see Appendix A.

26. For other sources used in this chapter and not referred to above, see the following items in the Bibliography: I, 5, 15; III, 7; IV, 2, 10, 11, 18, 30, 34, 37, 40, 47; V, 3, 60, 67, 86, 89; VI, 16. Also unpublished papers of the author on the ECSC, EDC, and EPC.

Chapter 5: The MRP and the Cold War

1. Einaudi and Goguel, *op. cit.*, pp. 123–30; *L'Aube*, May 26, 1950, p. 3.

2. *Terre Humaine*, January, 1951, pp. 38–53; February, 1951, pp. 79–80; March, 1951, p. 15.

3. *New York Times,* October 30, 1953, p. 4.

4. *L'Aube,* May 8, 1950, p. 1; September 7, 1950, p. 1; February 24–25, 1951, p. 6; *New York Times,* November 15, 1954, p. 1; *Le Monde,* January 30, 1954, p. 2.

5. *New York Times,* September 26, 1953, p. 1; *Vital Speeches,* November 1, 1953, pp. 41–47; *Journal des Débats,* February 13, 1952, pp. 677–83; *Terre Humaine,* March, 1952, p. 118.

6. *L'Aube,* May 2, 1950, p. 1; May 15, 1950, p. 4; May 22, 1950, p. 3; *Esprit,* February, 1954, p. 256.

7. *L'Aube,* April 18, 1950, p. 3; *New York Times,* June 26, 1953, p. 4; July 16, 1953, pp. 1, 7; January 21, 1954, p. 1; January 26, 1954, p. 4; January 29, 1954, p. 1; *U.N. World,* September, 1952, p. 41; *Esprit,* February, 1954, p. 260.

8. MRP *Brochures* (1945–46): "MRP, Parti . . . ," p. 27; *L'Aube,* December 29, 1950, p. 3; January 8, 1951, p. 1; *Manchester Guardian Weekly,* November 19, 1953, p. 2.

9. *Esprit,* June, 1950, pp. 1004–6; September, 1951, p. 375; *New York Times,* March 21, 1954, p. 3.

10. *Démocratie Nouvelle,* March, 1953, pp. 131–34; March, 1954, pp. 131–34; *Esprit,* January, 1951, pp. 102–21.

11. *Forces Nouvelles,* October 11, 1952, p. 1.

12. *Terre Humaine,* February, 1951, p. 4; November, 1952, p. 4; *New Statesman and Nation,* February 7, 1953, pp. 143–44; *Boston Herald,* December 14, 1953, p. 1. The French word *demander* only means "to ask."

13. *New Statesman and Nation,* February 13, 1954, p. 183; *U.N. World,* September, 1952, p. 25; *New York Times Magazine,* October 4, 1953, p. 9. Of those queried in the poll, 82 per cent knew no Americans.

14. *L'Aube,* May 19, 1950, p. 3; October 26, 1950, p. 1; November 1, 1950, p. 4; December 2–3, 1950, p. 1; *Terre Humaine,* March, 1951, p. 15. F. S. C. Northrop has emphasized the reaction of Western Europe against U.S. pressure for an EDC and apparent U.S. support for a crusade in his book *European Union and United States Foreign Policy* (New York: Macmillan Co., 1954).

15. *Terre Humaine,* February, 1952, pp. 1–7.

16. *Ouest France,* April 18–19, 1954, p. 1; *New York Times,* March 10, 1954, p. 1.

17. This stand was quite a contrast to the theory of "selective security" of neutralist Gilson. By this Gilson meant that France should be concerned with situations only where French national interests were directly involved. (*Le Monde,* August 2, 1950; *International Conciliation,* June, 1951, pp. 285–303.)

18. Despite the fact that Algeria is covered specifically in the scope of the NATO treaty (and thereby is indirectly involved in French foreign policy), it is not in the purview of this study, since it was at least until 1962 part of metropolitan France.

19. For other sources used in this chapter and not referred to above, see the following items in the Bibliography: I, 15; III, 5; IV, 25, 29, 30, 34; V, 6, 58, 61; VI, 6.

Chapter 6: MRP Policy Toward the French Union and North Africa

1. *Forces Nouvelles,* May 30, 1953, p. 12; June 5, 1954, p. 7.

2. *Terre Humaine*, August, 1953, pp. 53–56. See also Appendix A. Goguel
drew a historical parallel in citing the example of free trade imposed upon
France by Napoleon III in 1860, which had the effect of needling vested interests to such an extent that by 1869 it was an accomplished fact. (There is a
difference for Frenchmen, however, between the imposition of an economic
regime by a French ruler and by a supranational authority.)

3. *Christian Science Monitor*, December 27, 1954, p. 1; *New York Times*,
October 10, 1954; November 15, 1954, p. 11; December 26, 1954, Sect. IV,
p. 1; December 28, 1954, pp. 1, 8; January 21, 1955.

4. *L'Aube*, September 9–10, 1950, p. 1; September 30–October 1, p. 1;
Dorothy Pickles, *French Politics*, p. 195.

5. *L'Aube*, October 23, 1950, p. 4; October 24, 1950, pp. 1, 4; *Esprit*, January, 1953, pp. 81–87. See also Appendix A.

6. *L'Aube*, December 30–31, 1950, p. 6; *Nation*, March 15, 1952, p. 249;
New York Times Magazine, November 1, 1953, p. 13; *Spectator*, March 13,
1953, p. 302.

7. *New York Times*, January 11, 1954; *Le Monde*, April 29, 1954, p. 3; May
25, 1954, p. 7. But De Chevigné, MRP minister of war, had advised abandonment of Dien Bien Phu in February, 1954.

8. *Forces Nouvelles*, October 11, 1952, p. 1; *L'Aube*, January 8, 1951, p. 3.

9. *Forces Nouvelles*, May 30, 1953, p. 12; June 5, 1953, pp. 6–7; *New York
Times*, June 11, 1953, p. 1; June 26, 1953, p. 4; *Journal des Débats*, October
23, 1953, pp. 4580, 4613–15.

10. *Le Monde*, January 12, 1954, p. 5; February 11, 1954, p. 1; *New York
Times*, January 26, 1954, p. 4; January 29, 1954, p. 1; *Figaro*, April 26, 1954,
p. 1; *Forces Nouvelles*, May 8, 1954, p. 6.

11. *Le Monde*, February 26, 1954, p. 4; March 17, 1954, p. 1; April 16,
1954, p. 1; *Time*, September 13, 1954, p. 28.

12. Luethy, *op. cit.*, p. 224; *Occidente*, XI, No. 5 (1955), 367, 413.

13. MRP *Brochures* (1945–46): "Motions," pp. 6–13; *Nation*, June 3,
1950, p. 548 ff.; *New Statesman and Nation*, May 12, 1951, pp. 526–27; Taylor
Cole (ed.), *op. cit.*, pp. 646–48.

14. *L'Aube*, January 15, 1951, p. 1; March 19, 1951, p. 4; *News From
France*, June 15, 1951, p. 1; *L'Année Politique*, 1952, pp. 199, 230; *Vie Intellectuelle*, May, 1952, pp. 69, 74–80; *New York Times*, October 9, 1952,
p. 4; October 18, 1952, p. 5. Robert Schuman had taken the same line in November, 1952. See Annex to *Bulletin Quotidien* No. 2325, November 15, 1952.

15. *L'Aube*, June 10–11, 1950, p. 4; June 13, 1950, p. 1; *Forces Nouvelles*,
May 22, 1954, p. 6; June 5, 1954, p. 3.

16. *Commonweal*, July 22, 1949, p. 360; *L'Aube*, May 20–21, 1950, p. 2;
May 24, 1950, p. 2; July 17, 1950, p. 1; *International Organization*, May, 1953,
p. 203; *New York Times*, July 3, 1953, p. 1; July 4, 1953, p. 3; August 9, 1953,
p. 22; *Vital Speeches*, November 1, 1953, p. 44; Einaudi and Goguel, *op. cit.*,
p. 148.

17. See article by Paul Coste-Floret in *Politique*, May, 1948; also *Politique
Étrangère*, November, 1952, pp. 321–32; "Discours de Bidault devant le Conseil
de la République," October 19, 1953, p. 19.

18. *Journal des Débats*, November 18, 1953, pp. 5248–52; November 20,
1953, pp. 5354 ff.

19. *Forces Nouvelles*, October 11, 1952, p. 5; Pierre Pflimlin, *L'Europe et*

l'Union Française, p. 6; Annex à Procès-verbal, Assemblée de l'Union Française, No. 458, séance du 18 Décembre, 1952; *report of Vignes, Conseilleur.*

20. *Forces Nouvelles*, May 30, 1953, p. 12.

21. *Vie Intellectuelle*, December, 1951, p. 93; May, 1952, pp. 69, 74–80; *Esprit*, January, 1952, pp. 75–76; *Manchester Guardian Weekly*, September 18, 1952, p. 7.

22. *New York Times*, April 22, 1950, p. 27; *Esprit*, June, 1953, pp. 853–901; February, 1954, p. 255; *New York Times Magazine*, November 1, 1953, p. 28; *New Statesman and Nation*, January 23, 1954, p. 89; February 13, 1954, p. 183. See reference to other pressure groups in Robert Barrat, *Justice pour le Maroc*, pp. 150–54.

23. *La Nef*, March, 1953, pp. 7–9 ff.; *Terre Humaine*, April, 1953, pp. 1–4.

24. *Terre Humaine*, June–July, 1953, p. 156.

25. See Appendix A. See also Frederick Schuman, *War and Diplomacy in the French Republic*, p. 128; and John Eldred Howard, *Parliament and Foreign Policy in France*, p. 152 for the situation under the Third Republic; also *Revue Politique et Parlementaire*, February, 1951, p. 105. Between 1946 and 1951, the rate of continuity of cabinet ministers themselves never fell below 45 per cent. Pflimlin and Schuman had the longest tenure: 33 months. (*Journal of Politics*, November, 1952, pp. 643–58.)

26. *L'Aube*, September 18, 1950, p. 1; October 10, 1950, p. 3; November 1, 1950, p. 3; January 13–14, 1951, p. 1; *New York Times*, December 17, 1952, p. 10.

27. *The Times*, November 14, 1951, p. 6; December 14, 1951, p. 6; August 27, 1953, p. 6; *Terre Humaine*, December, 1951, pp. 126–31; September–October, 1953, pp. 11–27; *Esprit*, September, 1953, pp. 351–78; October–November, 1953, p. 658; *Le Monde*, January 27, 1954, p. 4; April 15, 1954, p. 4. Buron was an MRP leader who seemed to support the transfer to Moroccans of definite responsibilities. See *Témoignage Chrétien*, May 21, 1954, p. 1; *Reporter*, December 22, 1953, p. 19.

28. For other sources used in this chapter and not referred to above, see the following items in the Bibliography: I, 4, 6, 11; III, 3; IV, 8, 9, 12; V, 87; VI, 8, 20.

Chapter 7: MRP Tactics

1. Fréville (MRP), local leader and Mayor of Rennes, illustrated this transition from a theoretical to a practical approach. See Appendix A.

2. *Reconstruction*, January, 1954, pp. 1–5; April, 1954, p. 19.

3. Goguel's figures on the elections of 1951 are puzzling; elsewhere he said that 41.5 per cent of the MRP total vote came from the seventeen departments, while only 38.9 per cent of the total Communist vote came from them. (Einaudi and Goguel, *op. cit.*, p. 187.)

4. *Revue Politique et Parlementaire*, January, 1950, p. 306; April, 1951, p. 89; *New York Times*, June 25, 1950, p. 1; *Manchester Guardian Weekly*, June 29, 1950, p. 2.

5. Wright, *op. cit.*, pp. 86–88; *Nation*, August 6, 1949, p. 124.

6. Theodore White, *op. cit.*, pp. 11, 91.

7. Howard, *op. cit.*, p. 157; O. R. Taylor, *The Fourth Republic of France*, pp. 83, 212; Einaudi and Goguel, *op. cit.*, pp. 190–200, 214–18; Taylor Cole (ed.), *op. cit.*, pp. 663–64; *L'Aube*, May 11, 1950, p. 3; May 17, 1950, p. 3;

May 18, 1950, p. 3; January 8, 1951, p. 3; *New Statesman and Nation*, May 12, 1951, p. 527; *Current History*, January, 1951, p. 14; *Terre Humaine*, June, 1951, pp. 1–2; *New York Times*, June 18, 1951, p. 1; June 20, 1951, p. 26; *Journal of Modern History*, September, 1952, p. 283.

8. Wright, *op. cit.*, p. 78; *Nation*, October 29, 1949, p. 409; *L'Aube*, October 24, 1950, p. 4; *New York Times*, August 19, 1951, Sect. IV, p. 5; *Esprit*, November, 1951, pp. 663–64. *Entre la poire et le café* (sometimes *entre la poire et le fromage*) is an idiom translated here as "in extremities."

9. Duverger, *op. cit.*, p. 245; *L'Aube*, July 7, 1950, p. 3; *Esprit*, October, 1951, p. 575; *New York Times*, March 8, 1952, p. 1; December 23, 1952, p. 1. See also Appendix A.

10. The 88 seats that the MRP retained after the election of 1951 were further reduced to 70 in the next election of December, 1955. In 1958, the MRP was still hostile to electoral changes that would eliminate or alter the system of voting by departments. It did not have enough individual candidates or enough local strength to be very successful in a system based on electoral districts. (*New York Times*, February 26, 1958.)

11. *Terre Humaine*, May, 1952, p. 1–5.

12. *Vie Intellectuelle*, December, 1951, pp. 26–59; *Terre Humaine*, July, 1951, p. 37.

13. *L'Aube*, September 2–3, 1950, p. 1; *New York Times*, October 29, 1950, p. 8; *Terre Humaine*, December, 1951, pp. 70–73.

14. *New York Times*, September 25, 1952, p. 7; October 21, 1952, p. 1; *The Times*, October 22, 1952, p. 6; October 23, 1952, p. 6.

15. *New York Times Magazine*, November 1, 1953, p. 30; *Reporter*, December 22, 1953, p. 19; *Forces Nouvelles*, May 8, 1954, p. 1.

16. *L'Aube*, August 7, 1950, p. 3; August 21, 1950, p. 3; August 25, 1950, p. 3; January 22, 1951, p. 3; January 27–28, 1951, p. 6; *Esprit*, April, 1951, pp. 630–33; December, 1951, p. 840. However, see an intelligent approach by Buron in *Les Cahiers Économiques*, April, 1954, pp. 2–5 (which was also reflected in the author's interview with him; see Appendix A).

17. *Esprit*, March, 1953, p. 374; Fauvet, *op. cit.*, p. 182; Duverger, *op. cit.*, pp. 155–62; Einaudi and Goguel, *op. cit.*, pp. 204–5.

18. *The Times*, March 8, 1952, p. 6; *L'Année Politique*, 1952, pp. 16, 19, 25; *Manchester Guardian Weekly*, April 10, 1952, p. 2; April 17, 1952, p. 2; Campbell, "Discipline and Loyalty in the French Parliament during the Pinay Government," *Political Studies*, October, 1953, pp. 247–55.

19. *L'Année Politique*, 1952, pp. 202, 228; 1953, pp. 49–50; *Terre Humaine*, May, 1953, pp. 104–5; June–July, 1953, pp. 153–54; *Contemporary Review*, July, 1953, p. 9.

20. Upon inquiry, it appeared that the author was the only person of English or American nationality at the Congress. Correspondents were concentrating on the simultaneous critical Socialist Congress.

21. *New York Times*, November 15, 1954, p. 11; *Time*, September 13, 1954, p. 28; January 10, 1955, p. 18.

22. *Journal des Débats*, October 23, 1953, p. 4616.

23. *Ibid.*, February 16, 1952, p. 731; *L'Aube*, September 18, 1950, p. 1; October 9, 1950, p. 3.

24. *U.N. World*, September, 1952, p. 41; *Terre Humaine*, January, 1953, p. 122; *New York Times*, January 8, 1953, p. 6; January 30, 1953, p. 5; February 21, 1954, Sect. IV; *La Revue Politique*, April 25, 1953, p. 189.

25. *L'Aube*, November 3, 1950, p. 3; *U.N. World*, September, 1952, p. 41; *Forces Nouvelles*, May 30, 1953, p. 8.

26. But it is interesting that no MRP name appeared in the list of 169 Europeans who favored a widening of NATO in December, 1954.

27. *L'Aube*, September 23–24, 1950, p. 1; November 25–26, 1950, p. 1.

28. See Appendix A. See also *L'Aube*, November 25–26, 1950, p. 1; November 27, 1950, p. 3; *Forces Nouvelles*, October 11, 1952, p. 1; report of speech of P. H. Teitgen at Venice, April 29, 1953, pp. 6–7, 21–23.

29. *New York Times*, February 20, 1954, p. 3; *Le Monde*, February 6, 1954, p. 2; February 13, 1954, pp. 1, 2; February 26, 1954, p. 4; March 25, 1954, p. 3. See varying interpretations by Bidault and Schuman in *Le Monde*, April 8, 1954, p. 16 and *Revue Politique et Parlementaire*, March, 1954, p. 315. The author's interviews revealed that Le Brun Kéris and other *dirigeants* considered the question as one of fact rather than law.

30. *Journal des Débats*, February 12, 1952, pp. 648–50; November 17, 1953, pp. 5186, 5206–10.

31. *Ibid.*; *New York Times*, March 7, 1953, p. 8.

32. *Terre Humaine*, November, 1952, pp. 5–7.

33. See report of Teitgen's March 20, 1953, press conference. In that month, Bidault and Schuman suggested a national plebiscite. Schuman complained that with the predominance of opposition to the Treaty, it was a one-way contest. Ironically, he had done much to make it so. (*New York Times*, March 19, 1953, p. 9; March 20, 1953, p. 4.)

34. Report of Teitgen's March 20 press conference; *The Times*, June 11, 1953, p. 6; *New York Times*, June 11, 1953, p. 1.

35. For other sources used in this chapter and not referred to above, see the following items in the Bibliography: III, 4, 13; IV, 3, 7, 8, 10, 11, 30, 31, 34, 46; V, 3, 17, 36, 40, 41, 52, 67, 86, 105; VI, 5.

Chapter 8: Between Government and Parliament

1. *Journal des Débats*, February 16, 1952, pp. 739–44; February 19, 1952, p. 789; *New York Times*, February 17, 1952, p. 1; February 18, 1952, p. 9; February 19, 1952, p. 4.

2. *U.N. World*, September, 1952, pp. 23–24; *Vie Intellectuelle*, November, 1952, p. 114; *Spectator*, March 13, 1953, p. 302; Einaudi and Goguel, *op. cit.*, pp. 165–67. Bidault's ailment was partly due to a circulatory disorder called *tendance lypothymique*.

3. Pickles, *op. cit.*, p. 209; *L'Aube*, May 27–28, 1950, p. 1; March 19, 1951, p. 4; *Manchester Guardian Weekly*, June 22, 1950, p. 8; *Esprit*, December, 1951, pp. 842, 850; *The Times*, December 7, 1951, p. 5.

4. *Journal des Débats*, February 12, 1952, pp. 573–76; February 13, 1952, pp. 695, 699.

5. Pickles, *op. cit.*, pp. 202, 209; *L'Aube*, May 2, 1950, p. 1; July 29–30, 1950, p. 4.

6. White, *op. cit.*, p. 275; *L'Aube*, September 2–3, 1950, p. 1; September 4, 1950, p. 3; September 7, 1950, p. 1; February 15, 1951, p. 3.

7. *New York Times*, November 8, 1950, p. 30; November 25, 1950, p. 5; February 16, 1951, p. 8; *L'Aube*, February 15, 1951, p. 1; *Esprit*, November, 1951, p. 669. The numbers were set, however, not long thereafter.

8. *Terre Humaine*, February, 1951, p. 6; *The Times*, February 18, 1952, p. 4; *New York Times*, October 31, 1953, p. 16. See also Bidault, "Discours," October 29, 1953.

9. Pickles, *op. cit.*, p. 209; *L'Aube*, December 7, 1950, p. 3; December 21, 1950, p. 3; *Le Monde*, March 25, 1954, p. 3. The NATO arrangement in February, 1952, for joint sessions with the EDC would have brought Germany closer to the former. (*Manchester Guardian Weekly*, February 28, 1952, p. 1.) When the possibility arose of Germany's entrance into the Western European Union, Alfred Coste-Floret asked what could be expected of a security organization one of whose members had unsettled territorial claims. (Lerner and Aron, *op. cit.*, p. 176.) Of course, such an argument would have applied also to the EDC.

10. *Journal des Débats*, February 12, 1952, p. 635; *New York Times*, May 22, 1952, p. 1; *Manchester Guardian Weekly*, May 29, 1952, p. 1; *Spectator*, March 13, 1953, p. 303; *Christian Century*, December 30, 1953, p. 1515.

11. *New York Times*, December 30, 1952, p. 3; January 18, 1953, p. 1; February 8, 1953, p. 26; February 26, 1953, p. 1; March 1, 1953, p. 33; *Manchester Guardian Weekly*, March 5, 1953, p. 1; *Politique Internationale*, April, 1953, p. 468. For the six conditions in the protocols, see *New York Times*, January 10, 1953, p. 1; February 17, 1953, p. 26.

12. White, *op. cit.*, p. 263; *Politique*, April, 1947, p. 246; *L'Aube*, October 23, 1950, p. 4; *New York Times*, November 21, 1953, p. 1.

13. Luethy, *op. cit.*, pp. 361, 383; *The Times*, February 18, 1952, p. 4; *New York Times*, October 18, 1952, p. 1; January 31, 1954, p. 3; *Manchester Guardian Weekly*, September 24, 1953, p. 2; *Le Monde*, March 16, 1954, p. 4; April 13, 1954, p. 2.

14. *New York Times*, December 21, 1952, p. 20; February 25, 1953, p. 1; October 28, 1953, p. 1; *Le Monde*, January 7, 1954, p. 1.

15. *New York Times Magazine*, September 27, 1953, pp. 28–30.

16. *Loc. cit.* According to the *Nation* (September 25, 1954, p. 254), MRP "handouts" in early 1954 were that ratification of the EDC was a foregone conclusion, and that Bidault was indispensable at the Quai d'Orsay.

17. Howard, *op. cit.*, p. 81; *Esprit*, June, 1953, p. 853; *Le Monde*, February 26, 1954, p. 16; March 18, 1954, p. 16; *International Organization*, May, 1953, pp. 210–11.

18. *Journal des Débats*, February 13, 1952, pp. 686–89; February 19, 1952, p. 789.

19. A few days later, Bidault was careful to read out a correction in the February issue of *Revue Intellectuelle*. The wording in the January issue had been, as it developed, only a commentary on the Adenauer text taken from the extremist French journal *L'Observateur*. Billoux was unsuccessful in trying to get permission for a last word. (*Journal des Débats*, February 16, 1952, p. 746.)

20. *Ibid.*, pp. 791–93.

21. *Ibid.*, November 20, 1953, p. 5299; *Time*, September 13, 1954, p. 28.

22. *Journal des Débats*, November 17, 1953, pp. 5202–6, 5228.

23. *Vie Intellectuelle*, April, 1950, pp. 469–71; *Esprit*, March, 1953, p. 365; June, 1953, p. 862.

24. *Esprit*, March, 1951, p. 329; *New York Times*, February 12, 1952, p. 1; *Manchester Guardian Weekly*, February 14, 1952, p. 2.

25. *Le Monde*, April 14, 1954, pp. 1–2. The observation of the author on

the last point is that the Assembly took too many and too long recesses. Perhaps the reason for Bidault's reluctance to show the text lay in the fact that, although reports were that British Army units were to be stationed with EDC forces, among them one armored division, a perusal of the text of the United Kingdom statement reveals no reference to any specific units and also reveals qualifying clauses such as "where military considerations make this desirable." Contrast *Time*, April 26, 1954, with *The Department of State Bulletin*, April 26, 1954, pp. 619–21.

26. *New York Times*, October 29, 1950, p. 8; July 15, 1952, p. 4; *Journal des Débats*, November 20, 1953, pp. 5354 ff.

27. Partly due to the technicalities of a *question préalable*, Schuman, who had signed the Treaty, was not heard from at the time of defeat of the EDC in August, 1954.

28. For other sources used in this chapter and not referred to above, see the following items in the Bibliography: I, 4, 8, 10; II, 2; III, 5; IV, 2, 4, 6, 12, 15, 30, 48; V, 3, 55, 78, 86, 105.

Bibliography

I. MRP Documents and Publications

1. *Action Civique et Politique,* No. 2 (May, 1956), No. 6 (May, 1957), No. 13 (May, 1959), No. 16 (June, 1960), No. 19 (May–June, 1961). Reports at MRP National Congresses.
2. BIDAULT, GEORGES. "Discours devant le Conseil de la République," October 29, 1953.
3. DELFOSSE, GEORGES. "Notes: Scission du MRP." Unpublished.
4. LE BRUN KÉRIS, GEORGES. "Relations de l'Union Française et France Outre-Mer." Unpublished, January 25, 1953.
5. Mouvement Républicain Populaire. *Brochures,* 1945–46.
6. MRP Secretariat. "Plan de Travail: Relations de l'Union Européenne et France Outre-Mer." Unpublished.
7. ———. "Statuts Nationaux." Unpublished, May, 1950.
8. *MRP à l'Action.* Supplément No. 102, 25 Octobre 1950; Supplément, Décembre, 1953.
9. *Nouvelles Équipes Internationales* (Union des Démocrates Chrétiens). 8e Congrès, Tours, September 4–6, 1953.
10. PFLIMLIN, PIERRE. "L'Europe et l'Union Française." Unpublished, March 19, 1953.
11. POISSON, MAURICE. "Notes on Economic Relations with France Overseas." Unpublished address to Commission on France Overseas.
12. SIMMONET, MAURICE. "Report to the MRP National Committee, January 10, 1954, in name of Commission on Discipline." Unpublished.
13. ———. "Secretary-General's Report on MRP to Special National Congress." February, 1959.
14. TEITGEN, PIERRE-HENRI. "Press Conference." Unpublished, March 20, 1953.
15. ———. "Speech at Venice to Union Européenne des Féderalistes." Unpublished, April 30, 1953.
16. VIGNES, ALFRED. "Rapport à l'Assemblée de l'Union Française." Unpublished, December 18, 1952.

II. Public Documents

1. *Assemblée de l'Union Française,* No. 458 (1952), annexe à procès verbal, séance December 18, 1952.

2. *Assemblée Nationale,* No. 5404, annexe à procès-verbal, séance January 29, 1953, projet de loi.
3. *Consultative Assembly of the Council of Europe,* Compte Rendu Officiel, May 28, 1954.
4. *Journal Officiel de la République Française,* February, 1951, February, 1952.
5. ———, *Journal des Débats Parlementaires, Assemblée Nationale,* February 12–19, 1952, October 22–30, 1953, November 6–27, 1953.
6. Office of the High Commissioner for Germany. *Ninth Report on Germany.* 1951.

III. Newspapers

1. *L'Aube* (Paris), 1950, 1951.
2. *La Croix* (Paris), January–February, 1954.
3. *Figaro* (Paris), April–June, 1954.
4. *Forces Nouvelles* (Paris), 1952, 1953, 1954, 1957.
5. *The Times* (London), 1951–53.
6. *Manchester Guardian Weekly,* 1950–53.
7. *Le Monde* (Paris), January–May, 1954.
8. *The New York Times,* 1950–54.
9. *Nord-Éclair* (Lille), January–April, 1954.
10. *L'Observateur,* 1951–53.
11. *Ouest France* (Rennes), April, 1954.
12. *Témoignage Chrétien,* January–May, 1954.

IV. Periodicals

1. *America* (New York), 1953.
2. *L'Année Politique* (Paris), 1952, 1953.
3. *L'Année Politique et Economique* (Paris), 1953.
4. *Atlantic Monthly* (Boston), 1950–52.
5. *Bilans Hebdomadaires* (Paris), 1952, 1953.
6. *Bulletin Quotidien de Presse Étrangère* (Paris), 1951–53.
7. *Les Cahiers de Formation Politique* (Paris), 1949.
8. *Christian Century* (Chicago), 1953.
9. *Chroniques Sociales* (Paris), 1953.
10. *Chroniques de Politique Étrangère* (Brussels), 1950–52.
11. *Commonweal* (New York), 1952–53.
12. *Contemporary Review* (London), 1953.
13. *Démocratie Nouvelle* (Paris), 1953–54.
14. *La Documentation Catholique* (Paris), 1954.
15. *Droit Social* (Lyon), 1951.

16. *The Economist* (London), 1952.
17. *Écrits de Paris*, 1952.
18. *Esprit* (Paris), 1950–54.
19. *Foreign Policy Bulletin* (New York), 1952.
20. *Fortune* (New York), 1953.
21. *France Forum* (Paris), 1961.
22. *Jeune Europe* (Paris), 1954.
23. *Journal of Political Economy* (Chicago), 1953.
24. *Monde Nouveau Paru* (Paris), 1954.
25. *The Nation* (New York), 1949–53.
26. *La Nef* (Paris), 1952–54.
27. *The New Republic* (Washington), 1951, 1953.
28. *New Statesman and Nation* (London), 1950.
29. *The New Yorker*, 1953.
30. *News From France* (New York), 1946, 1950–51.
31. *Newsweek* (New York), 1951, 1952.
32. *Nouvelles de l'Europe* (Brussels), 1952.
33. *L'Observation Économique* (Paris), 1954.
34. *Politique* (Paris), 1947.
35. *Politique Internationale* (Paris), 1953.
36. *Reconstruction* (Paris), 1954.
37. *The Reporter* (New York), 1953, 1954.
38. *Review of Politics* (University of Notre Dame, South Bend, Ind.), 1953.
39. *Revue de Paris*, 1951.
40. *Revue Française des Sciences Politiques* (Paris), 1953.
41. *Revue Politique et Parlementaire* (Paris), 1950–51, 1953, 1954.
42. *Sondages* (Paris), 1952–54.
43. *Syndicalisme* (Paris), 1954.
44. *Terre Humaine* (Paris), 1951–53.
45. *Time* (New York), 1952, 1953.
46. *U.S. News & World Report* (Washington), 1953, 1954.
47. *Vie Intellectuelle* (Paris), 1950–54.
48. *Virginia Quarterly Review* (Charlottesville, Va.), 1953.

V. *Specific Sources*

1. ALMOND, GABRIEL. *The Appeals of Communism.* Princeton, N.J.: Princeton University Press, 1954.
2. ARENDT, HANNAH. *The Origins of Totalitarianism.* New York: Harcourt, Brace, and Company, 1951.
3. ARON, RAYMOND, and LERNER, DANIEL. *France Defeats the EDC.* New York: Frederick A. Praeger, 1957.
4. ARON, RAYMOND. "France in the Cold War," *Political Science Quarterly*, Vol. XXII, No. 1 (1951).

5. ———. "France Still the Third Republic," *Foreign Affairs*, October, 1951, p. 145.
6. ———. "French Public Opinion and the Atlantic Treaty," *International Affairs*, XXVIII, No. 1 (1952), 1.
7. ———. *Les Guerres en Chaines*. Paris: Gallimard, 1951.
8. BABOULÈNE, JEAN. "Une nouvelle étape de la CFTC," *Politique*, July–August, 1948, p. 664.
9. BARRAT, ROBERT. "Heroes of the French Church," *Commonweal*, January 8, 1954, p. 346.
10. ———. *Justice pour le Maroc*. Paris: Editions du Seuil, 1953.
11. BELLENAND, CLAUDE. "Le Plan Schuman," *Politique Internationale*, January, 1952.
12. BERNIS, JACQUES. "Les partis en quête de thèmes moteurs," *Politique*, July–August, 1948, p. 628.
13. BÉTHOUART, GENERAL. *La Peur du Risque et la CED*. Paris: La Plaque Tour, 1954.
14. BONNEFOUS, ÉDOUARD. *L'Europe en face de son Destin*. Paris: Editions du Grand Siècle, 1952.
15. BORNE, ÉTIENNE. *De Marc Sangnier à Marc Coquelin*. Toulouse: Privat, 1953.
16. BOURDET, CLAUDE. "The Socialists Balk," *Nation*, October 29, 1949, p. 408.
17. BOUSCAREN, ANTHONY T. "The MRP in French Governments, 1948–1951," *Journal of Politics*, XIV, No. 1 (1952), 104.
18. BOYLE, ANDREW. "Behind the Schuman Plan," *Catholic World*, CLXXII, No. 1030 (1951), 246.
19. BROGAN, DENNIS. "Two Nations in France," *Spectator*, May 29, 1953.
20. BURKS, R. V. "Catholic Parties in Latin Europe," *Journal of Modern History*, XXIV, No. 3 (1952), 269.
21. CALLENDER, HAROLD. "France Inhibited by Old Habits," *New York Times Magazine*, November 1, 1953.
22. ———. "The World as Seen from France," *New York Times Magazine*, March 2, 1952.
23. CAMPBELL, PETER. "Discipline and Loyalty in the French Parliament during the Pinay Government," *Political Studies*, Vol. I, No. 3 (1953).
24. DE CARMOY, GUY. *Fortunes de l'Europe*. n.p.: Domat, 1953.
25. CATROUX, GÉNÉRAL. "Union Française et Institutions Européennes," *International Conciliation*, November, 1953.
26. COCATRE-ZILGIEN, ANDRÉ. "La Confrontation Franco-Allemande," *Revue Politique et Parlementaire*, November, 1953, p. 245.
27. COSTE-FLORET, ALFRED. "Bilan et Perspectives d'une Politique Européenne," *Politique Étrangère*, November, 1952, p. 321.
28. COSTE-FLORET, PAUL, and GUENEDAL. *Construire l'Union Française*.

29. DARBON, MICHEL. *Le Conflit entre la Droite et la Gauche dans le Catholicisme Français, 1830–1953.* Toulouse: Privat, 1953.
30. DAVEY, ELIZABETH. *France in Crisis.* New York: H. W. Wilson Co., 1957.
31. DELBEZ, LOUIS. "La Communauté Européenne de Défense et les Principes du Droit Public," *Mouvement Européen,* April, 1954.
32. DELOURME, PAUL. *Trente-Cinq Années de Politique Religieuse ou l'Histoire de l'Ouest-Éclair.* n.p.: 1938.
33. DOMENACH, JEAN-MARIE. "Democratic Paralysis in France," *Foreign Affairs,* XXXVII (1958), 31.
34. DOURNES, PIERRE. "The MRP Today," *Commonweal,* July 22, 1949, p. 358.
35. "Douze Lettres sur la Communauté Européenne de Défense," *Mouvement Européen,* April, 1954.
36. DUVERGER, MAURICE. "Public Opinion and Political Parties in France," *American Political Science Review,* December, 1952, pp. 1069–78.
37. EINAUDI, MARIO, and GOGUEL, FRANÇOIS. *Christian Democracy in Italy and France.* South Bend, Ind.: University of Notre Dame Press, 1952.
38. FAUVET, JACQUES. *De Thorez à de Gaulle—Les Forces Politiques.* Paris: Éditions "Le Monde," 1951.
39. FONTANET, J. "La Situation Politique en France," *La Revue Politique,* April 25, 1953.
40. FRIEDLANDER, ERNST. "Adenauer and Schuman," *Spectator,* January 16, 1953, p. 69.
41. FURNISS, EDGAR S., JR. "French Attitudes toward Western European Unity," *International Organization,* III, No. 2 (1953), 199.
42. GABRIEL, RAYMOND. "Le Problème de la Sarre," *Politique Internationale,* No. 18 (July, 1953).
43. GAROSCI, ALDO. "La Francia e l'Europa," *Occidente,* XI, No. 5 (1955).
44. GAY, FRANCISQUE. *Les Démocrates d'Inspiration Chrétienne à l'Epreuve du Pouvoir: Mémoire Confidentiel.* Paris: Bloud et Gay, n.d.
45. (GENERAL XXX). *Réarmament Allemand et Défense Occidentale.* Aristide Quillet, 1954.
46. GENET. "Letter from Paris," *New Yorker,* October 10, 1953, p. 88.
47. GERAUD, ANDRE. "Insurrection Fades in France," *Foreign Affairs,* October, 1949, p. 30.
48. GILLIE, D. R. "France and the EDC," *Spectator,* March 13, 1953, p. 302.
49. GILSON, ÉTIENNE. "Le Système et l'Esprit," *Politique,* October, 1947, p. 673.

50. GOGUEL, FRANÇOIS. *France Under the Fourth Republic.* Ithaca, N. Y.: Cornell University Press, 1952.
51. ——. "Les Partis dans la Quatrième République," *Politique,* October, 1947, p. 685.
52. GOORMAGHTIGH, JOHN VICTOR. "European Integration," *International Conciliation,* No. 60 (February, 1953) p. 488.
53. GORDON, LINCOLN. "European Integration," *Yale Review,* September, 1955.
54. GORTAIS, EMILE. "La Signification Politique du Congrès de Toulouse," *Politique,* July–August, 1948, p. 611.
55. GUILLEMIN, HENRI, et al. *Les Chrétiens et la Politique.* Paris: Editions du Temps Présent, 1948.
56. HAVARD DE LA MONTAGNE, ROBERT. *Histoire de la Démocratie Chrétienne de Lamennais à Georges Bidault.* Paris: Amiot et Dumont, 1948.
57. HERALD, GEORGE W. "The Cabal that Rules France," *U.N. World,* August, 1953, pp. 8–12.
58. HOLTMAN, ROBERT A. "France: Multi-Party Difficulties," *Current History,* XX (1951), 11.
59. HOURDIN, GEORGES. "Devant la Crise Française," *Politique,* December, 1947, p. 865.
60. KAYSER, JACQUES. "Les Procédés Actuels de l'Information Compromettent-ils la Paix?", *Politique Étrangère,* January–March, 1952.
61. KNAPTON, ERNEST J. "France: Traditional Fears," *Current History,* XXIV (1953), 91.
62. KOEVES, TIBOR. "Meet Mr. Bidault," *U.N. World,* September, 1952, p. 23.
63. LAVERGNE, BERNARD. *Le Plan Schuman.* Paris: Librairie de Medicis, 1952.
64. ——. *Les Grands Problèmes de l'Union Française.* Paris: Edition de la Rose, 1953.
65. LE BRUN KÉRIS, GEORGES. *Mort des Colonies?* Paris: Le Centurion, 1953.
66. LEITES, NATHAN. *On the Game of Politics in France.* Palo Alto, Calif.: Stanford University Press, 1959.
67. LUETHY, HERBERT. *France Against Herself.* New York: Frederick A. Praeger, 1959.
68. MALLET, JACQUES. "L'Armée Européenne Pourquoi?", *L'Eveil de l'Europe,* No. 1, July, 1954.
69. MANSHOLT, S. L. "Toward European Integration: Beginnings in Agriculture," *Foreign Affairs,* October, 1952, pp. 106–13.
70. MAURIAC, FRANÇOIS. *Journal,* IV. 5 vols. Paris: B. Grasset, 1934–50.
71. McCORMICK, ANN O. "Now Europe Declares its Independence," *New York Times Magazine,* October 4, 1953, p. 9.

72. MICAUD, CHARLES A. "Stresses and Strains in France Today," *Virginia Quarterly Review*, XXVI, No. 3 (1950), 353.
73. MORAZE, CHARLES. *The French and the Republic*. Ithaca, N. Y.: Cornell University Press, 1958.
74. NOETHER, EMILIANA P. "*Political Catholicism in France and Italy*," *Yale Review*, Summer, 1955, p. 569.
75. PFLIMLIN, PIERRE. "Les Données Actuelles d'une Politique Économique Française," *Politique*, August–September, 1947.
76. PHILIP, OLIVER. *Le Problème de l'Union Européenne*. Paris: Edition de la Baconnière, 1950.
77. REUTER, PAUL. *La Communauté Européenne du Charbon et de l'Acier*. Paris: Librairie Générale de Droit et de Jurisprudence, 1953.
78. ROBINSON, KENNETH. "The Crisis of the French Union," *Occidente*, XI, No. 5 (1955).
79. SALVIN, MARINA. "Neutralism in France," *International Conciliation*, June, 1951, pp. 285–303.
80. DE SARCUS, PIERRE. "Le MRP a-t-il des ancêtres?", *Revue Politique et Parlementaire*, November, 1953, p. 248.
81. SAXE, J. W. "Herbert Luethy: 'The State of France.' " *Occidente*, XI, No. 5 (1955).
82. SCHERER, MARC. "Des Traités de Paris à la Conférence de Moscou," *Politique*, April, 1947.
83. SCHOENBRUN, DAVID. *As France Goes*. New York: Harper & Brothers, 1957.
84. SCHRAM, STUART S. "Behind the French Strikes," *Nation*, August 29, 1953, p. 164.
85. SCHUMAN, ROBERT. "Europe Will Go Forward to Unity," *New York Times Magazine*, September 27, 1953, p. 7.
86. ———. "France and Europe." *Foreign Affairs*, April, 1953, pp. 349–60.
87. SCHUMANN, MAURICE "France, the Key to European Peace," *Vital Speeches*, November 1, 1953, p. 40.
88. ———. "Léon Blum et la Paix," *Politique Étrangère*, June–July, 1950, p. 269.
89. SEDILLOT, RENE. "Letter to Americans," *Yale Review*, XLIII, No. 1 (1953).
90. THOMPSON, DAVID. "The Origins of Modern France," *Fortnightly*, n.s. 1014 (June, 1951), p. 379.
91. DEL VAYO, J. ALVAREZ. "French Politics in the Shadows," *Nation*, June 3, 1950, p. 548.
92. ———. "The Socialist Malaise," *Nation*, July 18, 1953, p. 45.
93. VISSON, ANDRÉ. "The Two Schumans of France," *Catholic World*, March, 1950, p. 436.
94. WERTH, ALEXANDER. "France after Dulles," *New Statesman and Nation*, February 7, 1953, p. 143.

95. ———. "The Lyons Congress," *New Statesman and Nation*, May 12, 1951, p. 526.
96. ———. "Neutralism, France's Common Ground," *Nation*, March 17, 1951, p. 247.
97. ———. "Neutralism Rejected," *Nation*, July 7, 1951, p. 5.
98. ———. "Who Rules France?", *New Statesman and Nation*, February 13, 1954, p. 183.
99. WHITE, THEODORE H. "Behind the Stalemate in French Politics," *New York Times Magazine*, May 31, 1953, p. 10.
100. ———. *Fire in the Ashes*. New York: William Sloan, Associates, 1953.
101. ———. "France: Politicians, Pressure Groups, and a New Face," *Reporter*, December 22, 1953, p. 18.
102. ———. "New Force in Europe, The Catholic Left," *Reporter*, September 16, 1952, p. 5.
103. ———. "Pinay to Mayer to Whom?", *Reporter*, March 3, 1953, p. 12.
104. WILLIAMS, PHILIP, and HARRISON, MARTIN. *De Gaulle's Republic*. London: Longmans, Green, 1960.
105. WILLIAMS, PHILIP. "The Compromisers," *Occidente*, XI, No. 5 (1955).
106. ———. "The French Elections," *Fortnightly*, September, 1951, p. 580.
107. WRIGHT, GORDON. "Catholics and Peasantry in France," *Political Science Quarterly*, Vol. LXVIII, No. 4 (December, 1953).
108. YATES, WILLARD ROSS. "Power, Principle, and the Doctrine of the MRP," *American Political Science Review*, June, 1958, p. 419.

VI. *General Sources*

1. CARRÈRE, BOURGIN, and GUÉRIN. *Manuel des Partis Politiques*. Paris: F. Rieder et Cie., 1924.
2. COLE, TAYLOR (ED.). *European Political Systems*. New York: Alfred A. Knopf, 1953.
3. DUVERGER, MAURICE. *Les Partis Politiques*. Paris: Libraire Armand Colin, 1951.
4. EARLE, EDWARD MEAD (ED.). *Modern France*. Princeton, N. J.: Princeton University Press, 1953.
5. FOUNDATION FOR FOREIGN AFFAIRS. *A Constitution for the Fourth Republic*. Washington, D.C.: Foundation Pamphlet No. 2, 1947.
6. HOWARD, JOHN ELDRED. *Parliament and Foreign Policy in France*. London: Cresset Press, 1948.
7. LIDDLEDALE, D. W. S. *The Parliament of France*. New York: Frederick A. Praeger, 1952.

8. MALEZIEUX, R., et ROUSSEAU, J. *La Constitution de la IVe République.* Paris: 2ᵉ édition, 1949.
9. MARABUTO, PAUL. *Les Partis Politiques et les Mouvements.* Paris: Recueil Sirey, 1948.
10. MIDDLETON, DREW. *The Defense of Western Europe.* New York: Appleton-Century-Crofts, 1952.
11. NEUMANN, SIGMUND. *Modern Political Parties.* Chicago: University of Chicago Press, 1950.
12. PICKLES, DOROTHY. *French Politics.* London: Royal Institute of International Affairs, 1953.
13. SCHUMAN, FREDERICK. *War and Diplomacy in the French Republic.* New York. Whittlesey House, 1931.
14. SEIGNOBOS, CHARLES. *Histoire Sincère de la Nation Française.* Paris: Les Éditions Rieder, 1933.
15. SIEGFRIED, ANDRÉ. *Tableau des Partis.* Paris: 1930.
16. SPAHR, MARGARET (ED.). *Readings in Recent Political Philosophy.* New York: The Macmillan Co., 1935.
17. TAYLOR, O. R. *The Fourth Republic of France.* London: Royal Institute of International Affairs, 1951.
18. THOMPSON, DAVID. *Democracy in France.* London: Oxford University Press, 1952.
19. WERTH, ALEXANDER. *France, 1940–1955.* New York: Henry Holt and Co., 1956.
20. WRIGHT, GORDON. *The Reshaping of French Democracy.* New York: Reynal and Hitchcock, 1948.

Index

Action Civique et Politique, 43
Adenauer, Konrad, 18, 128, 139–40
Ancel, Monsignor, 78
André, Pierre, 117
Anticlericalism, 15, 17
Aquinas, Thomas, 78
Aron, Raymond, 30, 54, 97, 147
Association Catholique de la Jeunesse
  Française, 37
Atlantic High Council, 52, 70
L'Aube, 8, 27, 32, 42–44, 67–69, 74,
  76, 84, 97, 113, 135–36
Auriol, Vincent, 104

Bacon, Paul, 38, 161
Bank of France, 96
Berlin Conference, 70, 75
Beuve-Méry, Hubert, 44, 72, 74, 106
Bichet, Robert, 38
Bidault, Georges, 8, 10, 12, 13, 17,
  18, 26, 30, 38, 41, 52, 54, 56, 57,
  59, 62–64, 66, 68–71, 73–77, 79,
  81–85, 87, 92, 96, 98–100, 104–7,
  110–12, 116–24, 126, 128, 130–35,
  138–41, 143–45, 155, 160
Billoux, François, 139
"Black Europe," 15–18
Bodin, Jean, 56
Bonn Contract, 121, 132, 140
Bonnefous, Edouard, 144
Bonnet, Georges, 84
Borne, Étienne, 15–16, 19, 23, 36,
  69–70, 73, 76, 78, 97, 104, 108,
  116, 122, 146–47
Bosson, Charles, 161
Bourdet, Claude, 72
Bouret, Henri, 115, 117
Briand, Aristide, 8, 142
Brittany, 12, 14–15, 29
Brogan, Dennis, 159
Bruce, David, 75
Buron, Robert, 23, 59, 81, 112–13,
  136, 161

Carrefour, 41
Catholic Church, 9, 19, 38, 64, 82
Catrice, Jean, 44, 74
Cercle du Patronat Chrétien, 40
Charpentier, René, 51–52, 161
Chrétiens progressistes, 8, 140
Christian democrats, 7–9, 19, 38, 62,
  108
Colin, André, 10, 23, 33, 37, 87, 113,
  161, 163–64, 166
Collier's, 77
Commission Nationale de Formation
  Politique, 159
Comité France-Maghreb, 97
Common Market, 55, 58, 60, 133,
  135, 161, 163, 166
Communists, 15, 21, 41, 66, 72, 75,
  82, 86, 105–6, 108, 117, 129, 139–
  40, 155, 159, 166
Confédération Française des Travail-
  leurs Chrétiens, 39, 103
Confédération Générale des Petites et
  Moyennes Entreprises, 40, 113
Connally, Tom, 77
Conseil National du Patronat Fran-
  çais, 40, 107
Corval, Pierre, 98
Coste-Floret, Alfred, 29, 93, 121–22,
  132, 146
Coste-Floret, Paul, 85, 90, 93, 94,
  104, 121, 165
Council of Europe, 51, 93–94, 136
La Croix, 42

Darbon, Michel, 19
Déat, Marcel, 162
De Gaulle, Charles, 14, 53, 54, 71,
  89, 106, 110, 111, 113, 157–61,
  164
Démocratie Chrétienne Française, 155
Denis, André, 25, 26, 85–86, 103,
  114, 116, 160
Dien Bien Phu, 84, 86

193